Francis Frith's

Around Chichester

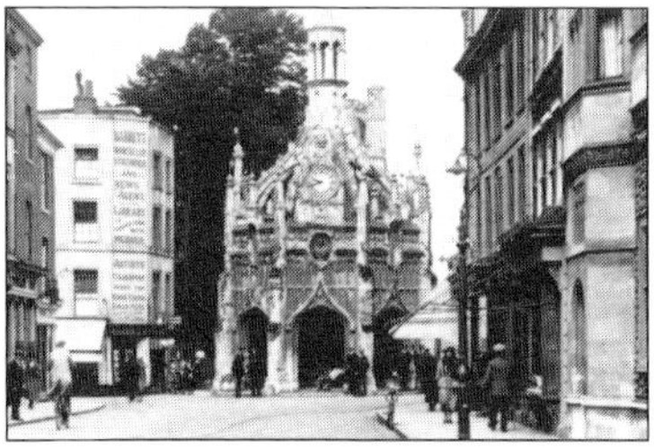

PHOTOGRAPHIC MEMORIES

Francis Frith's
AROUND CHICHESTER

Martin Andrew

THE FRANCIS FRITH COLLECTION
FRITH
BOOK CO

First published in the United Kingdom in 1999 by
Frith Book Company Ltd

British Library Cataloguing in Publication Data

Around Chichester
Martin Andrew
ISBN 1-85937-089-6

Frith Book Company Ltd
Frith's Barn, Teffont,
Salisbury, Wiltshire SP3 5QP
Tel: +44 (0) 1722 716 376
Email: frithbook.co.uk

Printed and bound in Great Britain

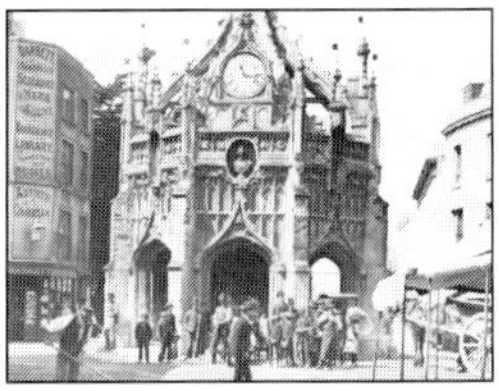

Contents

FRANCIS FRITH: *Victorian Pioneer*

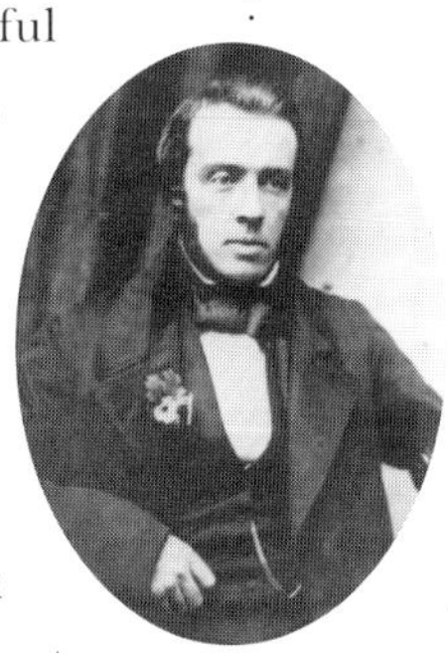

FRANCIS FRITH, Victorian founder of the world-famous photographic archive, was a complex and multitudinous man. A devout Quaker and a highly successful Victorian businessman, he was both philosophic by nature and pioneering in outlook.

By 1855 Francis Frith had already established a wholesale grocery business in Liverpool, and sold it for the astonishing sum of £200,000, which is the equivalent today of over £15,000,000. Now a multi-millionaire, he was able to indulge his passion for travel. As a child he had pored over travel books written by early explorers, and his fancy and imagination had been stirred by family holidays to the sublime mountain regions of Wales and Scotland. 'What a land of spirit-stirring and enriching scenes and places!' he had written. He was to return to these scenes of grandeur in later years to 'recapture the thousands of vivid and tender memories', but with a different purpose. Now in his thirties, and captivated by the new science of photography, Frith set out on a series of pioneering journeys to the Nile regions that occupied him from 1856 until 1860.

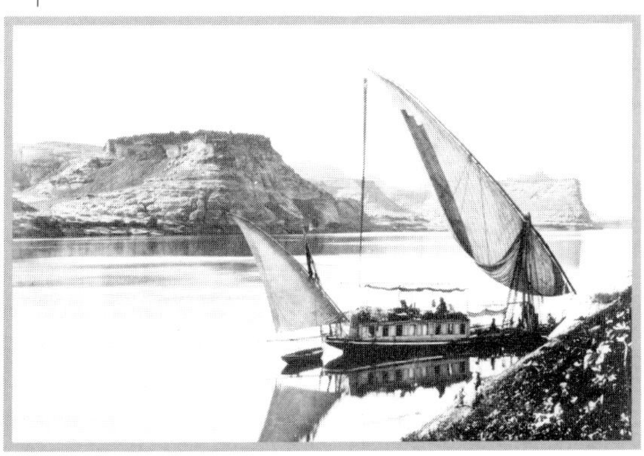

INTRIGUE AND ADVENTURE

He took with him on his travels a specially-designed wicker carriage that acted as both dark-room and sleeping chamber. These far-flung journeys were packed with intrigue and adventure. In his life story, written when he was sixty-three, Frith tells of being held captive by bandits, and of fighting 'an awful midnight battle to the very point of surrender with a deadly pack of hungry, wild dogs'. Sporting flowing Arab costume, Frith arrived at Akaba by camel seventy years before Lawrence, where he encountered 'desert princes and rival sheikhs, blazing with jewel-hilted swords'.

During these extraordinary adventures he was assiduously exploring the desert regions bordering the Nile and patiently recording the antiquities and peoples with his camera. He was the first photographer to venture beyond the sixth cataract. Africa was still the mysterious 'Dark Continent', and Stanley and Livingstone's historic meeting was a decade into the future. The conditions for picture taking confound belief. He laboured for hours in his wicker dark-room in the sweltering heat of the desert, while the volatile chemicals fizzed dangerously in their trays. Often he was forced to work in remote tombs and caves where conditions were cooler. Back in London he exhibited his photographs and was 'rapturously cheered' by members of the Royal Society. His reputation as a photographer was made overnight. An eminent modern historian has likened their impact on the population of the time to that on our own generation of the first photographs taken on the surface of the moon.

Venture of a Life-Time

Characteristically, Frith quickly spotted the opportunity to create a new business as a specialist publisher of photographs. He lived in an era of immense and sometimes violent change. For the poor in the early part of Victoria's reign work was a drudge and the hours long, and people had precious little free time to enjoy themselves.

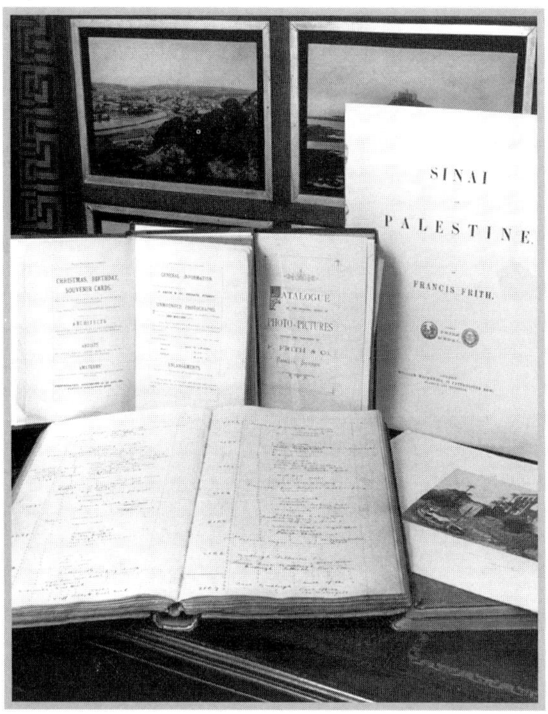

Most had no transport other than a cart or gig at their disposal, and had not travelled far beyond the boundaries of their own town or village. However, by the 1870s, the railways had threaded their way across the country, and Bank Holidays and half-day Saturdays had been made obligatory by Act of Parliament. All of a sudden the ordinary working man and his family were able to enjoy days out and see a little more of the world.

With characteristic business acumen, Francis Frith foresaw that these new tourists would enjoy having souvenirs to commemorate their days out. In 1860 he married Mary Ann Rosling and set out with the intention of photographing every city, town and village in Britain. For the next thirty years he travelled the country by train and by pony and trap, producing fine photographs of seaside resorts and beauty spots that were keenly bought by millions of Victorians. These prints were painstakingly pasted into family albums and pored over during the dark nights of winter, rekindling precious memories of summer excursions.

The Rise of Frith & Co

Frith's studio was soon supplying retail shops all over the country. To meet the demand he gathered about him a small team of photographers, and published the work of independent artist-photographers of the calibre of Roger Fenton and Francis Bedford. In order to gain some understanding of the scale of Frith's business one only has to look at the catalogue issued by Frith & Co in 1886: it runs to some 670

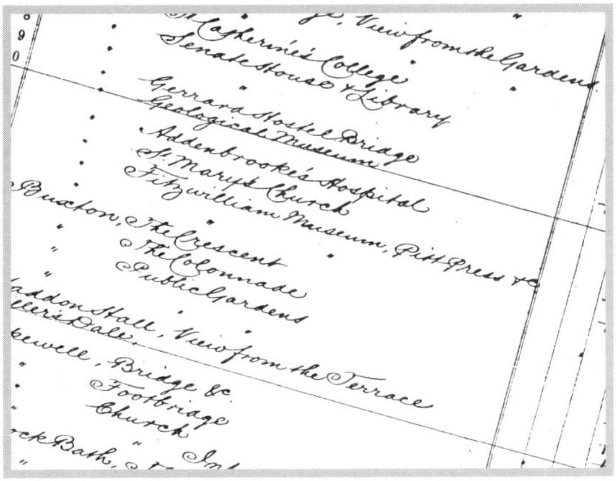

pages, listing not only many thousands of views of the British Isles but also many photographs of most European countries, and China, Japan, the USA and Canada – note the sample page shown above from the hand-written *Frith & Co* ledgers detailing pictures taken. By 1890 Frith had created the greatest specialist photographic publishing company in the world, with over 2,000 outlets – more than the combined number that Boots and WH Smith have today! The picture on the right shows the *Frith & Co* display board at Ingleton in the Yorkshire Dales. Beautifully constructed with mahogany frame and gilt inserts, it could display up to a dozen local scenes.

POSTCARD BONANZA

The ever-popular holiday postcard we know today took many years to develop. In 1870 the Post Office issued the first plain cards, with a pre-printed stamp on one face. In 1894 they allowed other publishers' cards to be sent through the mail with an attached adhesive halfpenny stamp. Demand grew rapidly, and in 1895 a new size of postcard was permitted called the court card, but there was little room for illustration. In 1899, a year after Frith's death, a new card measuring 5.5 x 3.5 inches became the standard format, but it was not until 1902 that the divided back came into being, with address and message on one face and a full-size illustration on the other. *Frith & Co* were in the vanguard of postcard development, and Frith's sons Eustace and Cyril continued their father's monumental task, expanding the number of views offered to the public and recording more and more places in Britain, as the coasts and countryside were opened up to mass travel.

Francis Frith died in 1898 at his villa in Cannes, his great project still growing. The archive he created continued in business for another seventy years. By 1970 it contained over a third of a million pictures of 7,000 cities, towns and villages. The massive photographic record Frith has left to us stands as a living monument to a special and very remarkable man.

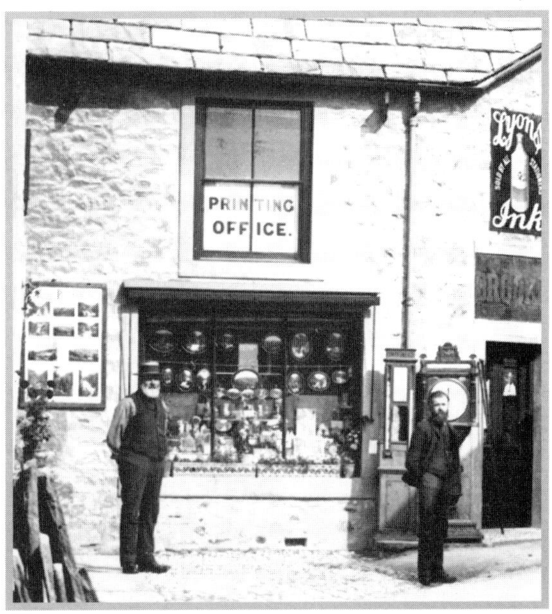

Frith's Archive: *A Unique Legacy*

Francis Frith's legacy to us today is of immense significance and value, for the magnificent archive of evocative photographs he created provides a unique record of change in 7,000 cities, towns and villages throughout Britain over a century and more. Frith and his fellow studio photographers revisited locations many times down the years to update their views, compiling for us an enthralling and colourful pageant of British life and character.

We tend to think of Frith's sepia views of Britain as nostalgic, for most of us use them to conjure up memories of places in our own lives with which we have family associations. It often makes us forget that to Francis Frith they were records of daily life as it was actually being lived in the cities, towns and villages of his day. The Victorian age was one of great and often bewildering change for ordinary people, and though the pictures evoke an impression of slower times, life was as busy and hectic as it is today.

We are fortunate that Frith was a photographer of the people, dedicated to recording the minutiae of everyday life. For it is this sheer wealth of visual data, the painstaking chronicle of changes in dress, transport, street layouts, buildings, housing, engineering and landscape that captivates us so much today. His remarkable images offer us a powerful link with the past and with the lives of our ancestors.

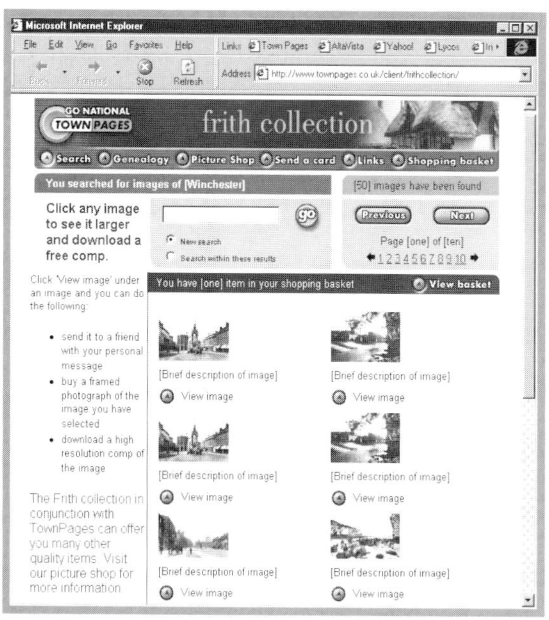

See Frith at www. francisfrith.co.uk

Today's Technology

Computers have now made it possible for Frith's many thousands of images to be accessed almost instantly. In the Frith archive today, each photograph is carefully 'digitised' then stored on a CD Rom. Frith archivists can locate a single photograph amongst thousands within seconds. Views can be catalogued and sorted under a variety of categories of place and content to the immediate benefit of researchers. Inexpensive reference prints can be created for them at the touch of a mouse button, and a wide range of books and other printed materials assembled and published for a wider, more general readership - in the next twelve months over a hundred Frith local history titles will be published! The day-to-day workings of the archive are very different from how they were in Francis Frith's time: imagine the herculean task of sorting through eleven tons of glass negatives as Frith had to do to locate a particular sequence of pictures! Yet the archive still prides itself on maintaining the same high standards of excellence laid down by Francis Frith, including the painstaking cataloguing and indexing of every view.

It is curious to reflect on how the internet now allows researchers in America and elsewhere greater instant access to the archive than Frith himself ever enjoyed. Many thousands of individual views can be called up on screen within seconds on one of the Frith internet sites, enabling people living continents away to revisit the streets of their ancestral home town, or view places in Britain where they have enjoyed holidays. Many overseas researchers welcome the chance to view special theme selections, such as transport, sports, costume and ancient monuments.

We are certain that Francis Frith would have heartily approved of these modern developments, for he himself was always working at the very limits of Victorian photographic technology.

The Value of the Archive Today

Because of the benefits brought by the computer, Frith's images are increasingly studied by social historians, by researchers into genealogy and ancestory, by architects, town planners, and by teachers and schoolchildren involved in local history projects. In addition, the archive offers every one of us a unique opportunity to examine the places where we and our families have lived and worked down the years. Immensely successful in Frith's own era, the archive is now, a century and more on, entering a new phase of popularity.

The Past in Tune with the Future

Historians consider the Francis Frith Collection to be of prime national importance. It is the only archive of its kind remaining in private ownership and has been valued at a million pounds. However, this figure is now rapidly increasing as digital technology enables more and more people around the world to enjoy its benefits.

Francis Frith's archive is now housed in an historic timber barn in the beautiful village of Teffont in Wiltshire. Its founder would not recognize the archive office as it is today. In place of the many thousands of dusty boxes containing glass plate negatives and an all-pervading odour of photographic chemicals, there are now ranks of computer screens. He would be amazed to watch his images travelling round the world at unimaginable speeds through network and internet lines.

The archive's future is both bright and exciting. Francis Frith, with his unshakeable belief in making photographs available to the greatest number of people, would undoubtedly approve of what is being done today with his lifetime's work. His photographs, depicting our shared past, are now bringing pleasure and enlightenment to millions around the world a century and more after his death.

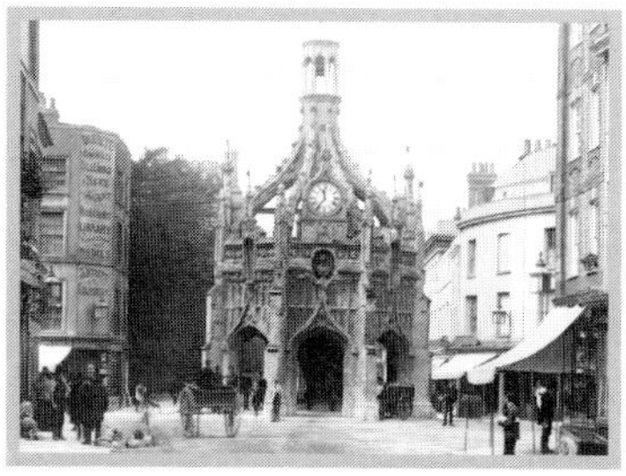

CHICHESTER – *An Introduction*

CHICHESTER IS A FINE CITY that wears its extremely long history remarkably lightly. Though now considerably expanded beyond its walled core, and surrounded by suburbs and a dual carriageway by-pass on the A27, enough of the city as it was in about 1850 remains to give even the most unobservant visitor pause for thought. From the South Downs and from many places on the flat Sussex coastal plain the city, the county town of West Sussex, is a very real presence through its cathedral spire.

Chichester started life as a Roman city, founded in the 1st century AD following the conquest of much of the Celtic island which the Romans called Britannia. The invading army commanded by Aulus Plautus Nepos was welcomed by the local king in 43 AD, whose palace at nearby Fishbourne was his reward. This, only unearthed in 1960, nearly nineteen centuries after it was built, was one of the largest and most opulent Roman buildings north of the Alps: it was a palace fit for a king, with elaborately planned rooms, extensive underfloor central heating, stone buildings around a richly planted courtyard and a second court with gardens running down to the sea. The first major evidence exposed was a mosaic floor; many more mosaics of the highest artistic quality, together with extensive building foundations, are contained in special buildings erected to protect them, while part of the courtyard gardens have been restored. A visit here should be an essential part of any tour of the area.

Tiberius Claudius Cogidubnus, King of the Regnenses, presided over a prosperous region from his palace, which was built around 75 AD. He was, of course, a client king, but had the title of King and Imperial Legate. A mile eastwards the town of Chichester was established, and it became a successful one. It was named Noviomagus Regnensium, meaning the new market place of the Regnenses tribe, and was laid out on the normal Roman plan of north-south and east-west roads intersecting in the centre of town. These roads still survive almost on their original alignment, but the minor roads within the town do not; this seems to indicate that in later times the city shrank within its walls, with settlement only along the axial roads.

Around 200 AD the city acquired stone defensive walls to replace the earth bank and ditch, with bastions added later. Although they are much added to and refaced and rebuilt during medieval times the walls survive, adapted in the 18th century into rampart walks along much of the northern half of the city. Good views of the south-west section can be seen across playing fields; it is only in the south-east quarter, or 'Quadrant' as these sectors are known locally, that much of the wall has disappeared or is hidden. A walk along these wall walks is an excellent way of getting

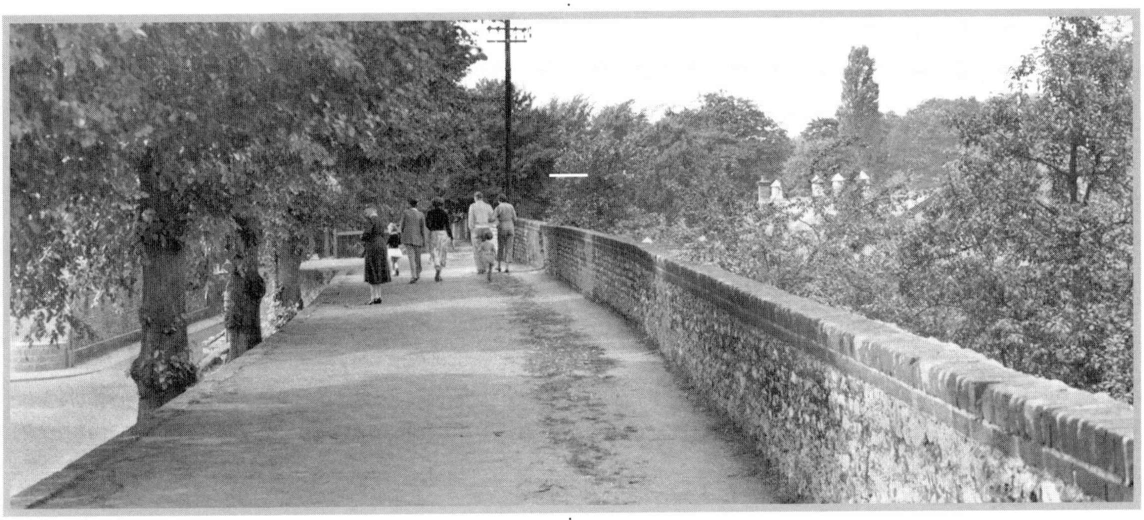

a feel for the city's layout.

Any excavation within the city wall seems to turn up Roman material in abundance, and a fuller picture is being formed of this golden era in the city's history. It acquired its present name from the next wave of invaders, the English, or to be more accurate the Anglo-Saxons. In 477 AD the Saxon warlord Aelle and his sons Cissa, Cymen and Wlencing arrived in three ships. Landing near West Wittering they seized Noviomagus and established the Kingdom of the South Saxons, nowadays known as Sussex. The old Roman city was given to Cissa and it became known as Cissas ceastre, or Cissa's camp: hence Chichester.

The Anglo-Saxon kingdoms waxed and waned, but a key event was the landing of St.Wilfred at Selsey in 681 AD. He converted the local king and aristocracy to Christianity, and he is reputed to have established the bishopric of Sussex at Selsey. Sussex played a further role in history when Harold, the Anglo-Danish Earl of Wessex, prayed and feasted at Bosham, where the church still survives, before setting off on his ill-fated trip to Normandy in 1064. Apparently he promised to support William of Normandy's claim to the English throne upon the death of King Edward the Confessor. However, Harold became king in 1066; William invaded, won the hard-fought Battle of Hastings in which Harold died, and, as they say, the rest is history. However, Chichester profited immediately in townscape terms, for the bishopric's seat was moved from Selsey to Chichester in 1075.

Ralph Luffa, Bishop from 1091 to 1123, was responsible for building the bulk of the cathedral, a splendid Norman building, with the west part of the nave completed by Seffrid I in the 1130s. The cathedral had a disastrous fire in 1187 which led to a new east end and much refacing, as well as stone vaults being added throughout. Two towers were blown down in 1210, and the rebuilt central tower received a towering 271-foot spire around 1300. The spire and tower collapsed in 1861; the rubble was photographed at the time, but when the spire was rebuilt by Sir George Gilbert Scott, the architect of St.Pancras Station, the Foreign Office and the Albert Memorial, he added six feet to its height. There was an old rhyme whose prophecy was fulfilled by the tower falling: 'If Chichester tower do fall, in England there's no king at all'. There was indeed no king, for Queen Victoria was on the throne at the time.

The other medieval building that cannot be missed (in any sense of the word) is the market cross, erected at the centre of the town where the axial roads intercept. Donated by Bishop Edward Storey in 1501, it is a wonderfully elaborate structure that has survived the arrival of the motor car and lorry and, in a now predominantly pedestrianised city centre, has seen off a challenger that all over the country has swept away historic buildings that have the temerity to obstruct motor traffic.

The cathedral and close occupy much of the south-west quadrant, and give it a distinctly medieval character. The close is entered by a medieval gateway from South Street. As well as the cathedral itself, many of the houses and buildings within its confines contain medieval work, including the Vicar's Close, the Bishop's Palace and the Chantry. Elsewhere within the walls there are several medieval parish churches, and in the north-west quadrant stands the great choir of the Grey Friars, built between 1269 and 1282 on land donated by Richard, Earl of Cornwall. This fine building is situated in what is now a park given by the Duke of Richmond and Gordon in 1918 as a war memorial and for the citizens to enjoy. To the north of Greyfriars is a mound, now municipalised, which is all that remains of the castle motte which was demolished in 1217.

So, in this city the Romans gave us its main streets and walls and occasional discoveries

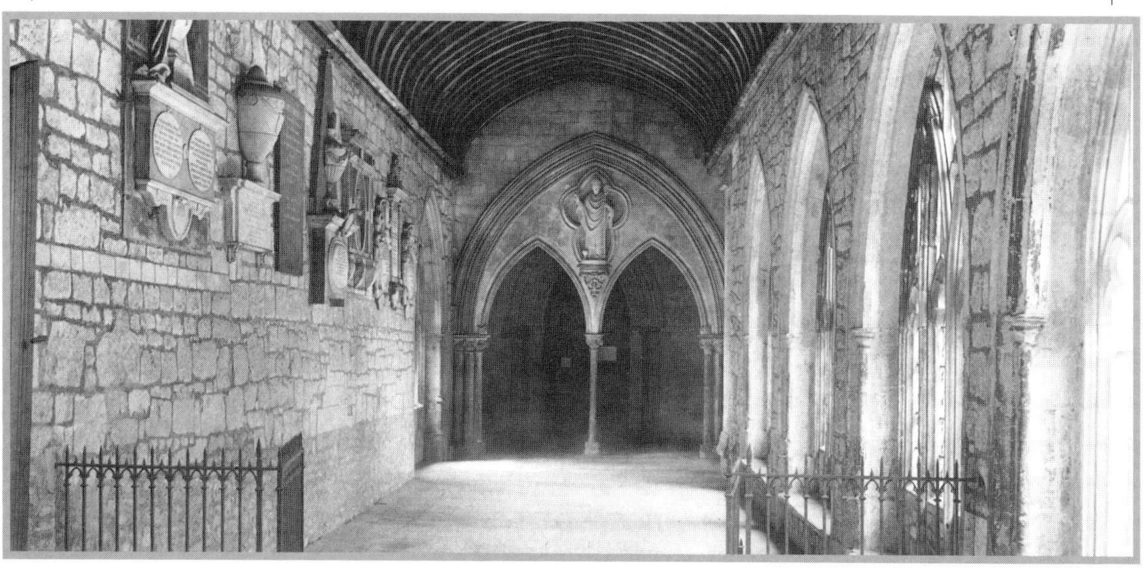

such as the mosaic visible below the floor of the cathedral. The Anglo-Saxons gave the city its name, and from the Middle Ages we have the great cathedral including its gateways and buildings in the close, Greyfriars, the medieval churches, St Mary's Hospital and much of the rebuilt city walls. Alas, all four medieval city gatehouses went in the late 18th century.

However, much of the external character of the houses both in the close and in the city streets and lanes is Georgian, and predominantly brick. It is this phase in the history of the city that gave it its distinctive character. I know there has been much destruction since the war, and some poor rebuilding, but such is the cohesiveness of the city that most visitors come away with a favourable impression. The worst destruction has been in the north-west quadrant, and some stretches of North and East Street show their scars; but wandering in the Pallants in the south-east quadrant, or around St Martin's Square in the north-east, is deeply satisfying for those visitors who value a good provincial Georgian townscape. Admittedly, many of these Georgian and early 19th-century fronts hide Tudor and 17th-century timber-framed houses, but the overwhelming feeling in this fine city is of Georgian brick and sliding sash windows. There are, of course, many cottages with casement windows within the walls, but the general architectural character demonstrates clearly a great era of wealth for this city when the citizens, local gentry and merchants prospered on corn, cattle and milling.

The city in its prosperous heyday acquired all the civilised and civic buildings necessary to corporate and city life: a Council House in 1731, Assembly Rooms in 1787, a Market House in 1807 and a theatre in 1791. In 1832 a Corn Exchange was built, a massively confident Greek Doric temple in West Street, now a hamburger restaurant. The opening of the branch canal to the Portsmouth-Arun Canal in 1823 further benefited the town's trade, and also allowed more goods to reach the city via the canal basin with its warehouses. Later in the century boats and barges laden with coking coal fed the town gas works, strategically placed by the canal basin. Ironically, the Chichester Branch canal survives, together with the stretch of the Portsmouth-Arun between Hunston, where the branch joined it, and the outlet into Chichester Harbour: the rest of the canal is now only earthworks, long since dried-up.

The 20th century has seen bad things happen to the city: misguided demolitions (what town has not suffered these?), some bomb damage during the Second World War, and considerable expansion into the surrounding fields, some of it poor, some of it better. It has also seen many good things: the Festival Theatre, pedestrianisation and traffic calming in the centre, and an increased awareness of the value of the city's splendid architecture and character. The city is by-passed by the A27, in fact one of the earliest by-passes in the country.

The overall impression left on the visitor is of a city on a humane scale, with buildings of quality which yet do not give a stand-offish impression. It is an intimate city, a feeling emphasised by its cathedral, which is one of the smaller medieval ones: nothing too showy and crucially in keeping with the town. The way through its close via the cloisters and

Canon Lane is integral to pedestrian flow through the city: the cathedral is not aloof from the bustle of city life, and at lunchtime in particular many citizens come to eat their sandwiches in part of the gardens of the Bishop's Palace, a haven surrounded by high Tudor battlemented mellow brick walls.

I have known and loved the city for over thirty years. I studied the Norman architecture of the cathedral for my M.Phil thesis; coincidentally, the other major church featured in this book, Boxgrove Priory, was the subject of my MA thesis. The last two chapters of this book are intended to provide short itineraries to the surrounding countryside. The first covers the villages surrounding Chichester Harbour, including Fishbourne and its Roman palace and Bosham, the second takes you to the east up onto the Downs and Goodwood racecourse, then downhill into Boxgrove. These two tours will, I hope, give you a flavour of the riches to be found in the area. Above all, I commend Chichester itself.

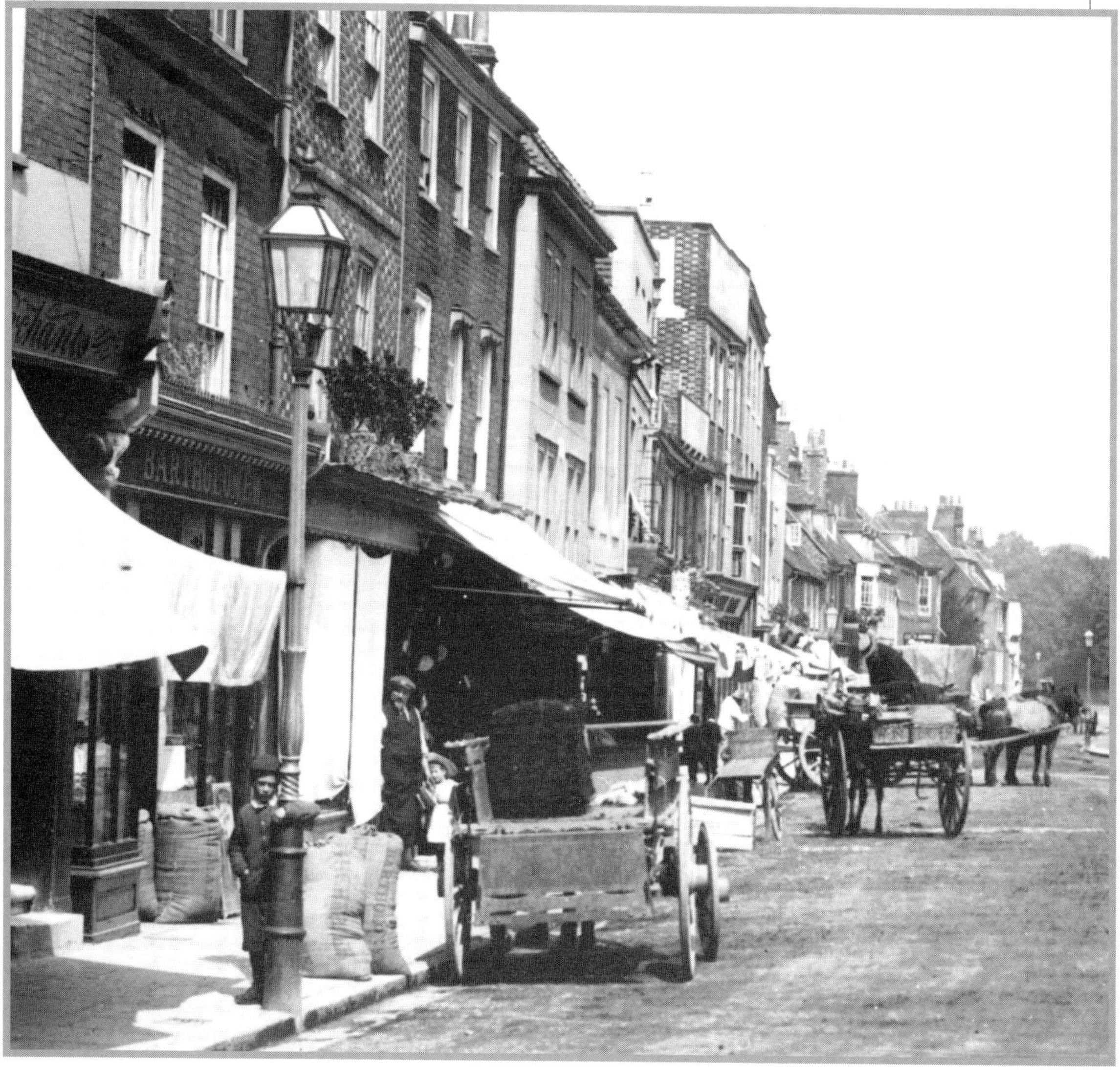

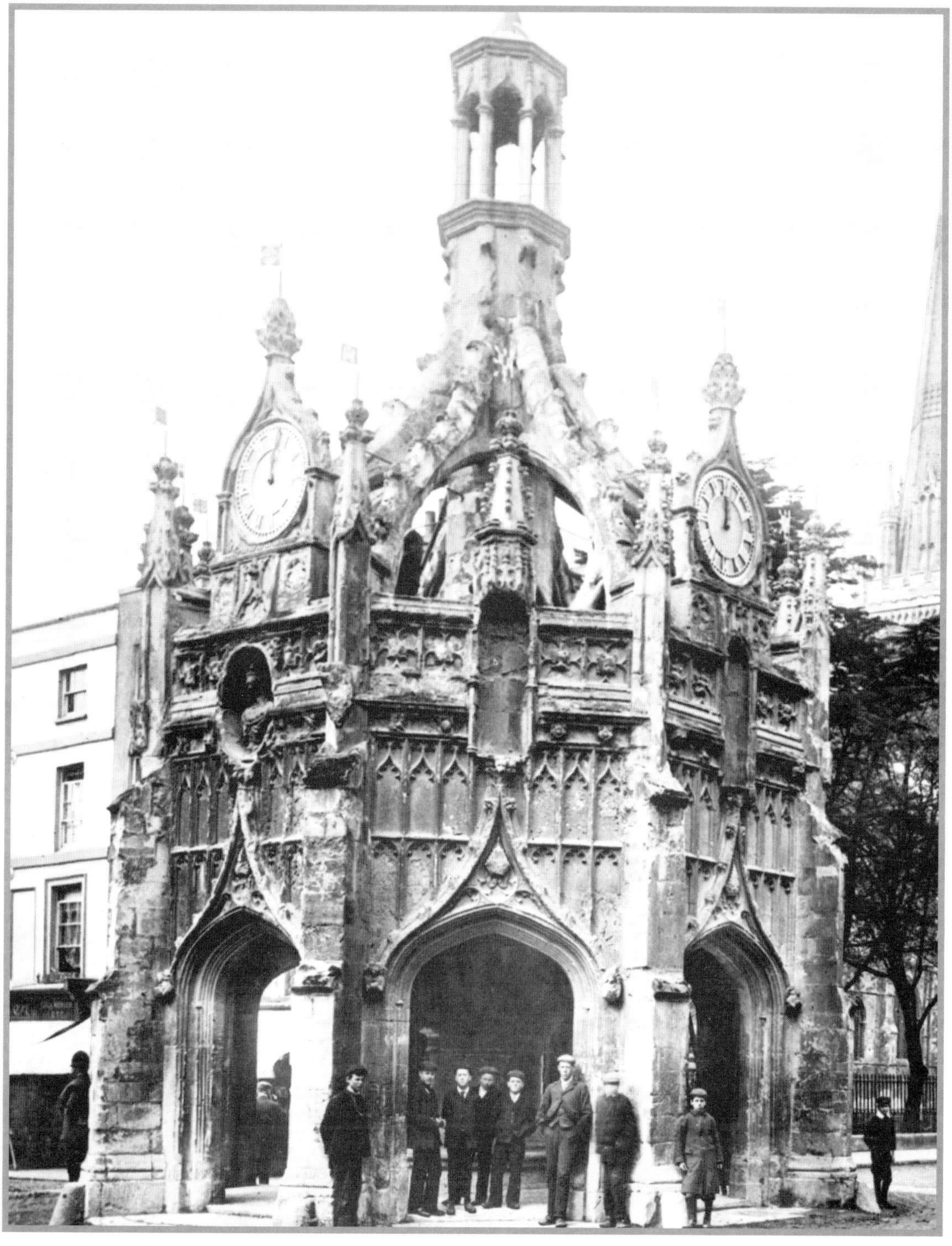

Market Cross 1903 50923
Chichester's wonderful medieval market cross dominates the cityscape, positioned as it is at the site where, nearly two thousand years ago, the east-west and north-south Roman roads intersected in the centre of the new-walled town of Noviomagus Regnensium.

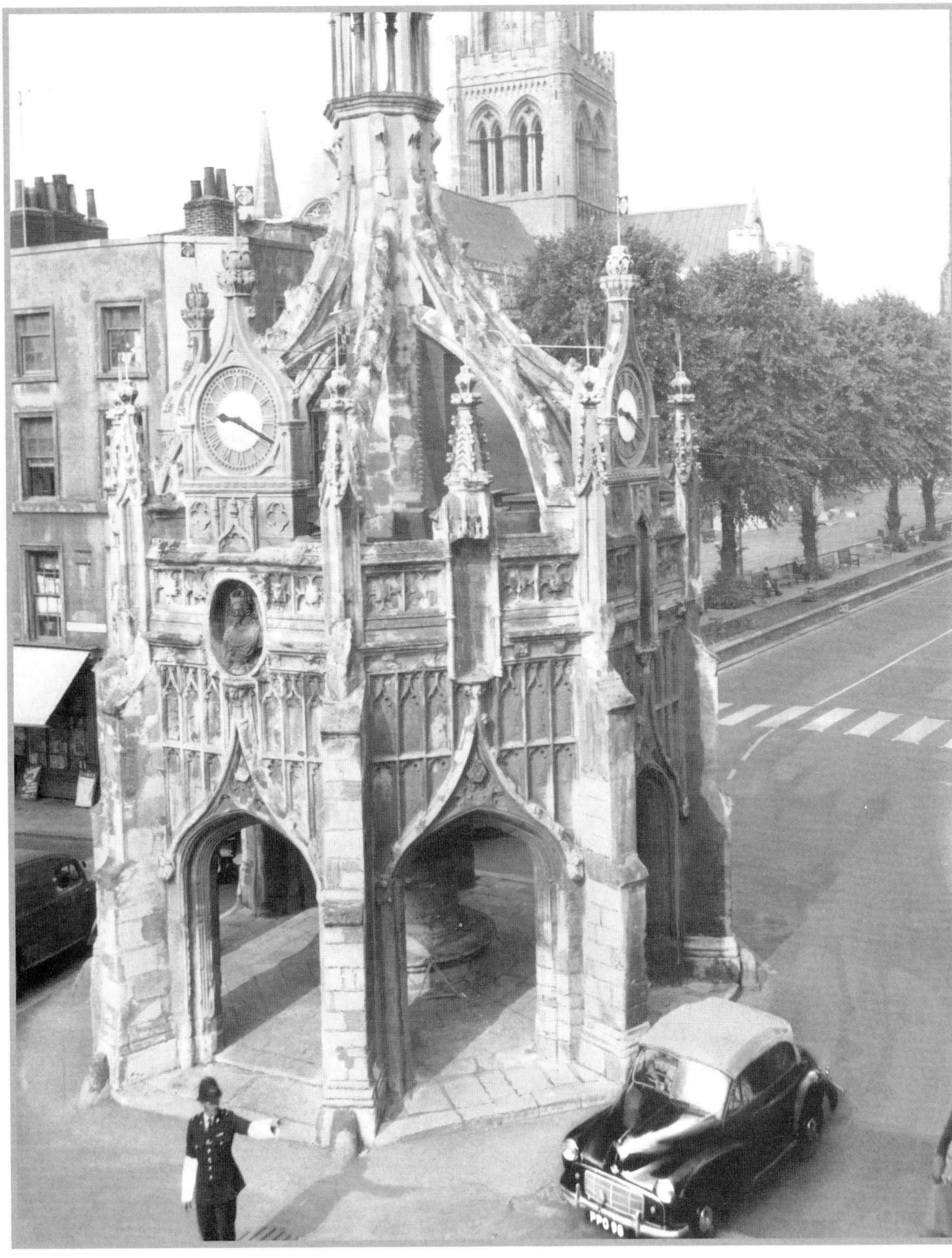

MARKET CROSS & THE CATHEDRAL c1960 C84074

The market cross was the gift in 1501 of the then bishop of Chichester, Edward Storey, so that the poorer people could sell their goods unhindered; he bought its site for £10 from the city corporation. The policeman on point duty is no longer needed here, for the area is now mostly pedestrianised.

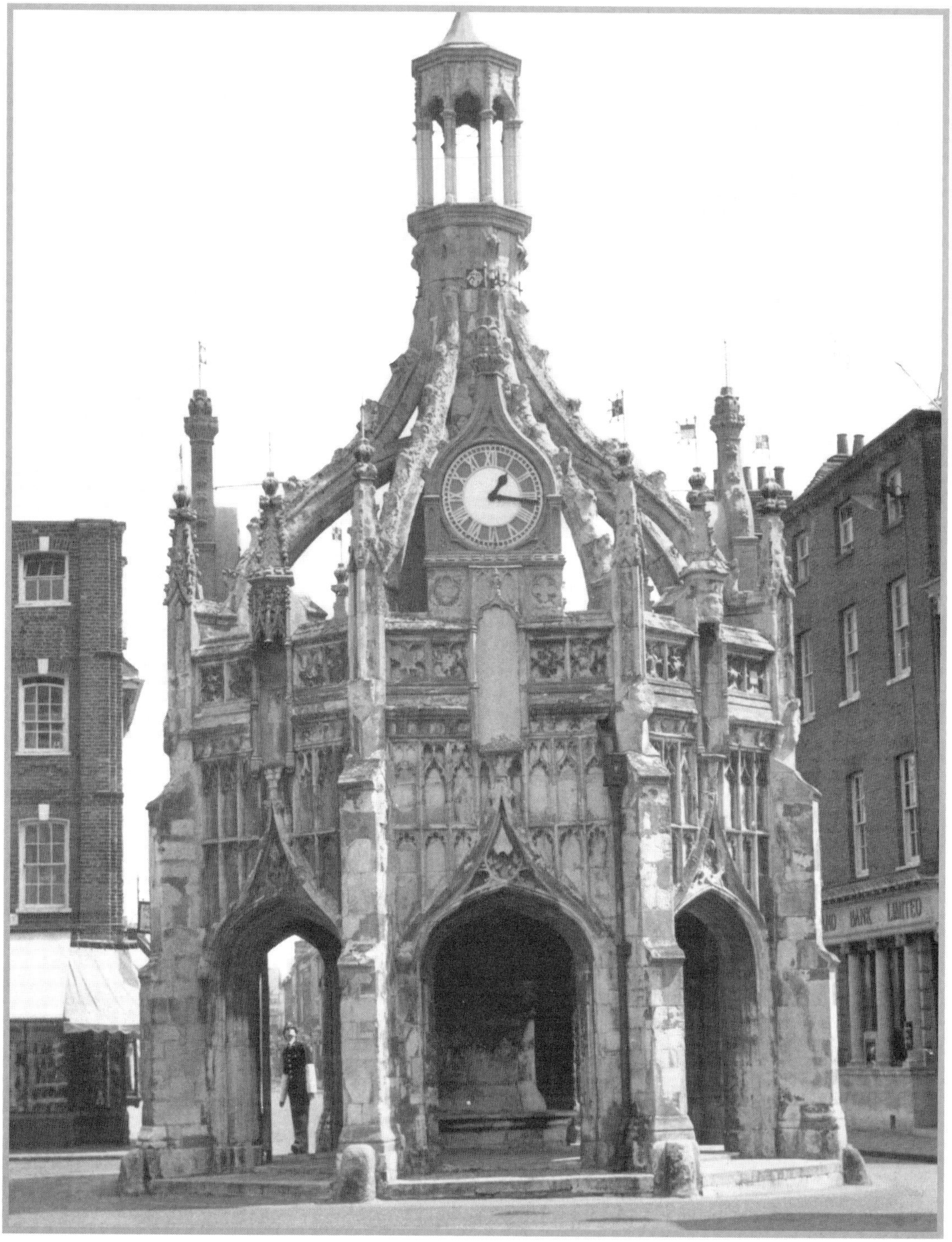

MARKET CROSS c1960 C84076

Octagonal in plan, the Cross has an ogeed arch to each facet, four facing down the principal streets. Elaborate flying buttresses rise from pinnacles to support a Georgian cupola, which replaced a stone structure with saints in niches. The original much-worn stone bench around the central column is still popular today.

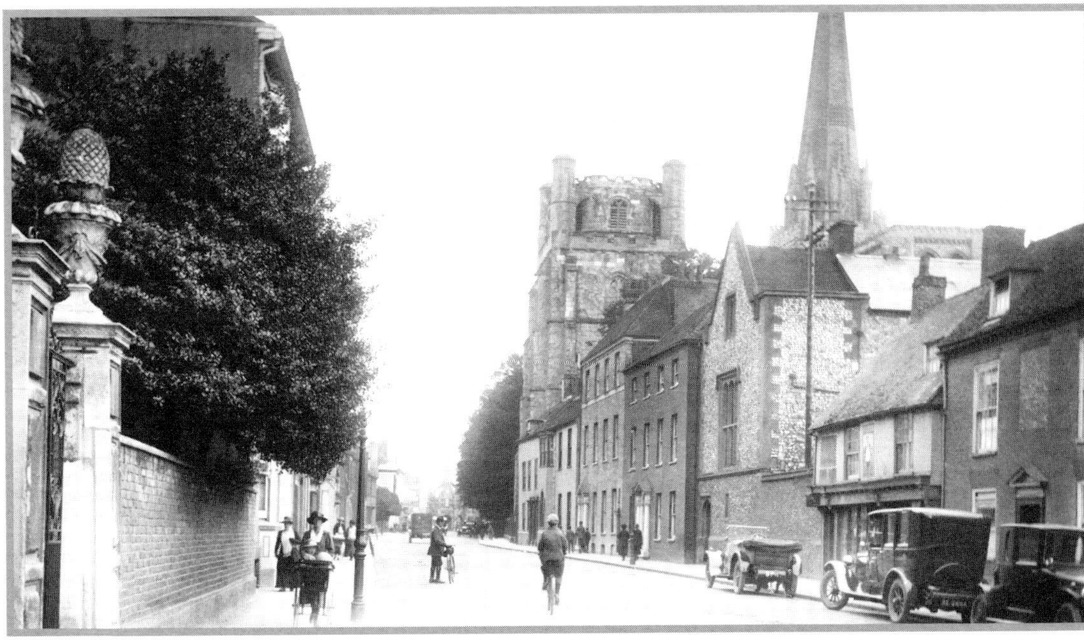

WEST STREET 1923 73656

West Street runs arrow-straight towards the Cross, with the Prebendal School on the right and the cathedral it supplies with choristers beyond, while on the left the great stone pineapples belong to Edes House, a fine mansion of 1696. The wall was rebuilt in stone, lower and further back, in the 1930s.

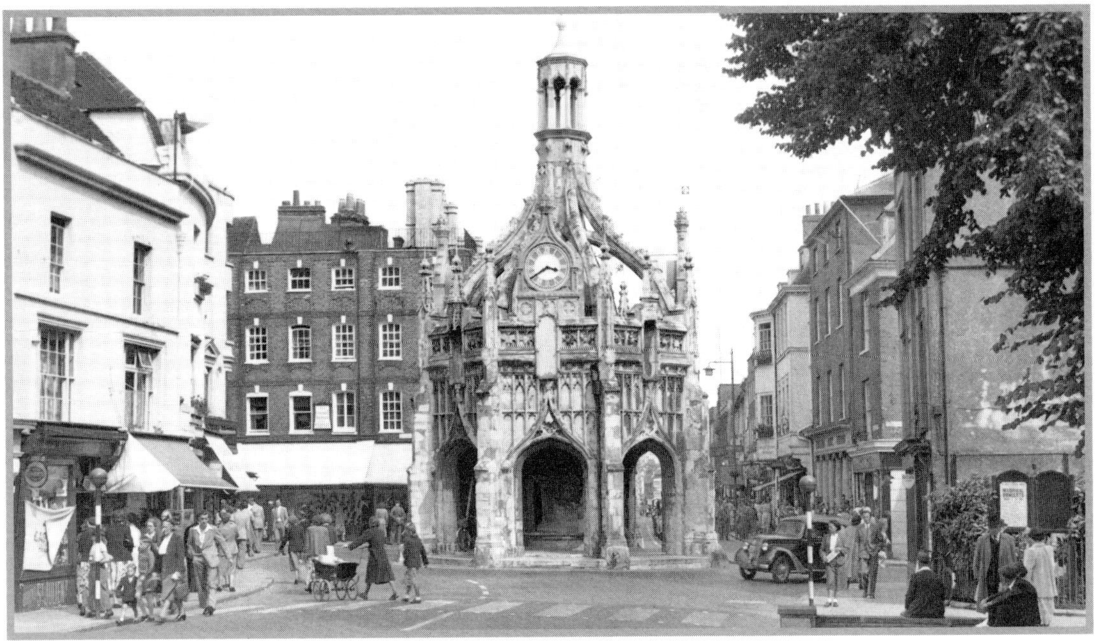

THE MARKET CROSS FROM WEST STREET c1955 C84024

In this view the early Georgian building to the left of the Cross, No.1 East Street, then the Cathedral Tea House, still stands with its original sash windows. The traffic pressure in the 1950s, even on a busy shopping day, is sufficiently slight for pedestrians to walk in the roadway.

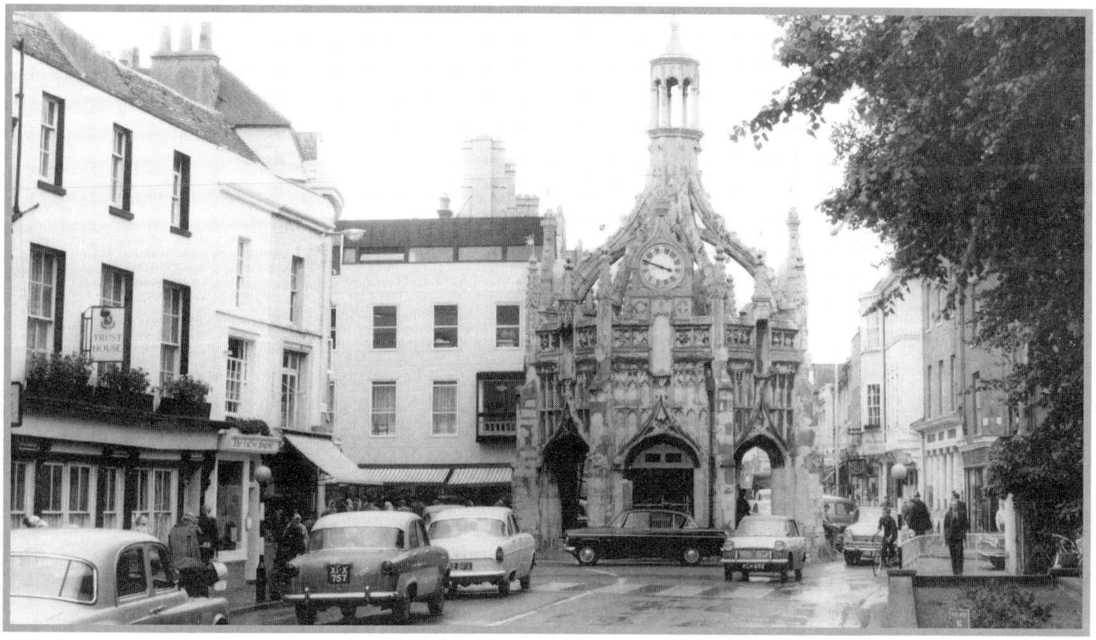

THE CROSS c1965 C84124
Ten years after view No C84024 the traffic looks more hectic, and the police have put up 'No waiting' signs. It is even sadder that the Georgian brick building to the left of the Cross has been demolished to make way for a bland replacement - one of many such demolitions the city suffered in the 1960s and 1970s.

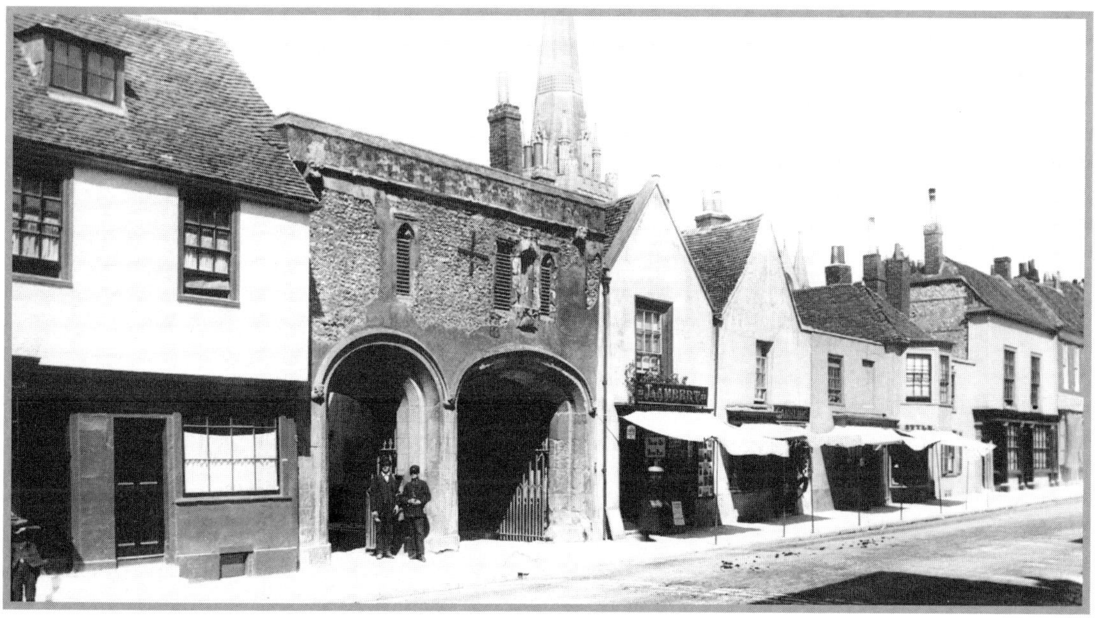

CANON LANE, SOUTH STREET 1890 22623
Our tour now moves up South Street towards the Cross. Remarkably little has changed here, apart from replaced shop fronts. The medieval gateway into Canon Lane and the Cathedral Close, since restored, was built in the late 1520s, while the houses to the right conceal 15th-century work behind their frontages, predating the gateway itself.

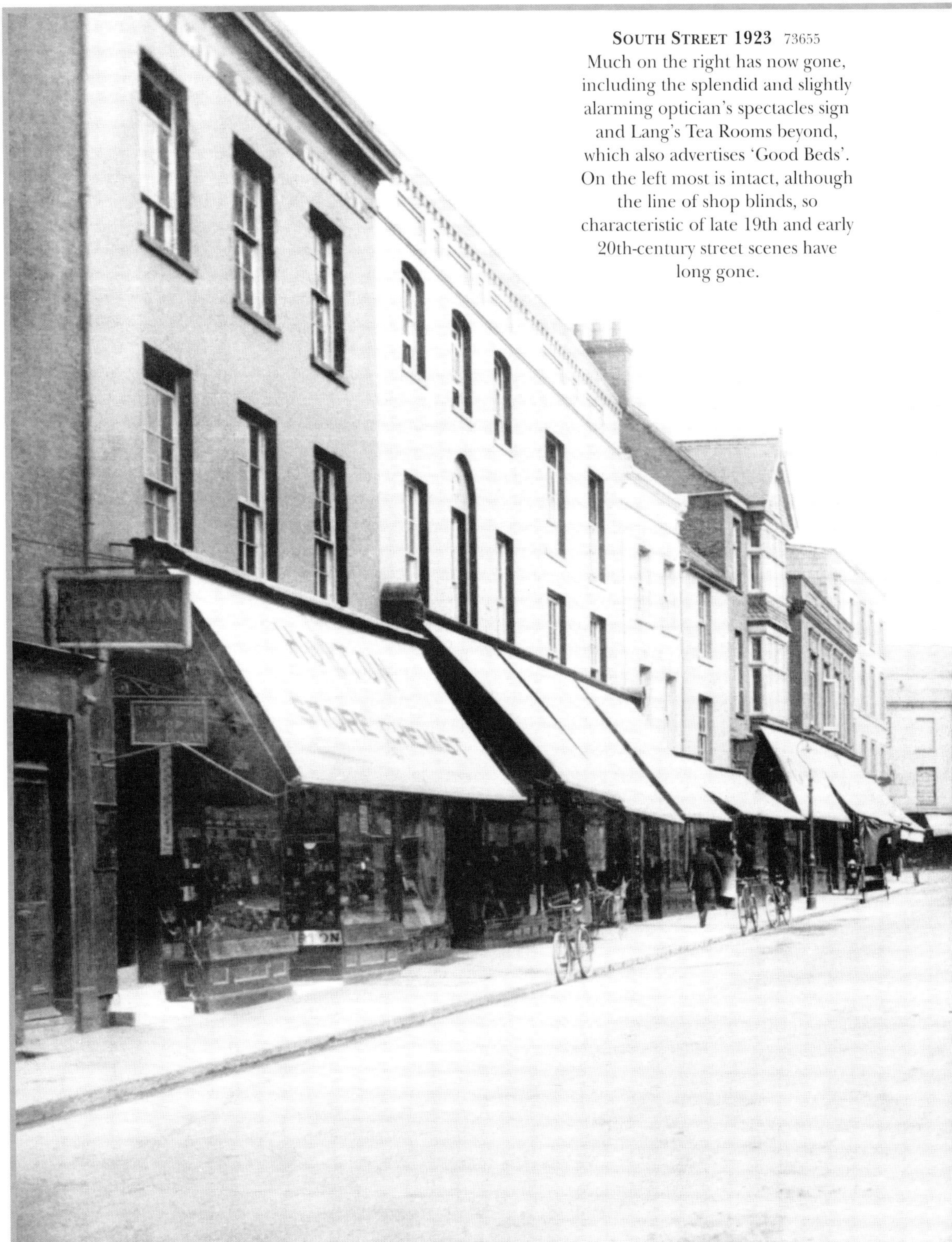

SOUTH STREET 1923 73655
Much on the right has now gone, including the splendid and slightly alarming optician's spectacles sign and Lang's Tea Rooms beyond, which also advertises 'Good Beds'. On the left most is intact, although the line of shop blinds, so characteristic of late 19th and early 20th-century street scenes have long gone.

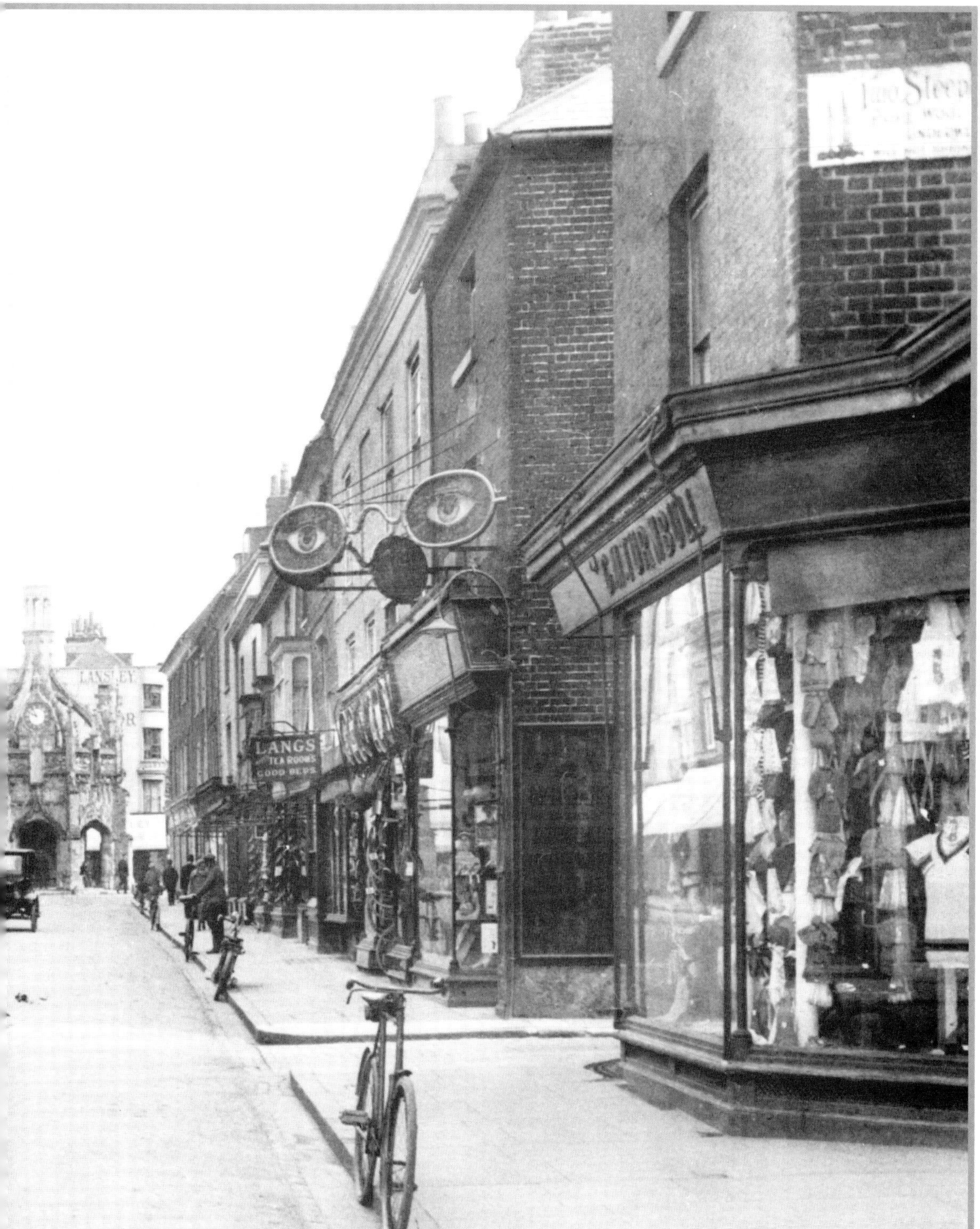
LANGS
TEA ROOMS
GOOD BEDS

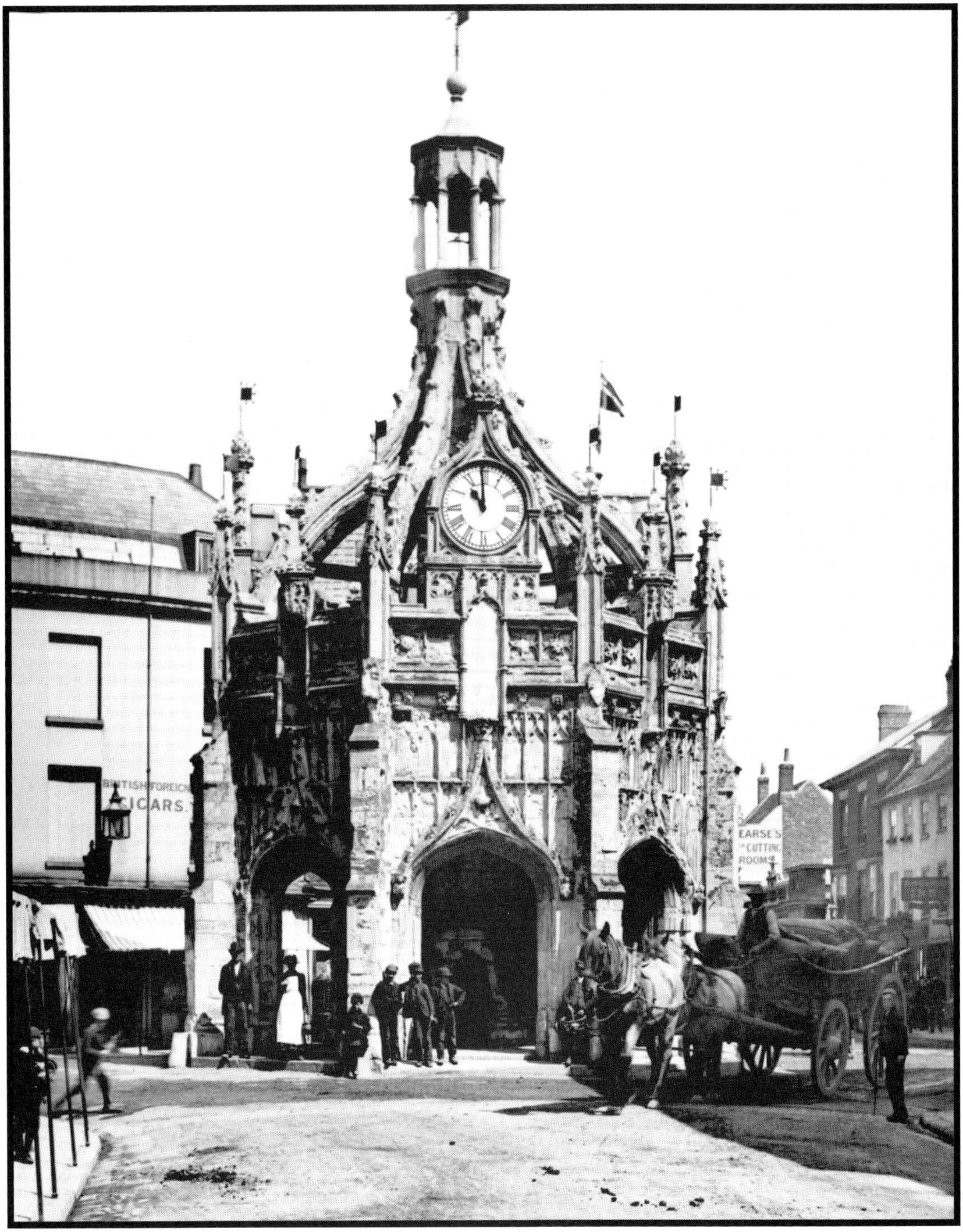

MARKET CROSS 1890 22615
Closer to the Cross, where a laden Sussex waggon is entering South Street, this interesting view shows the Market House facade in North Street beyond, to the right of Pearse's Cutting Rooms. This photograph was taken ten years before John Nash's single-storey building received an upper storey in stone, which can be seen in view No C84010.

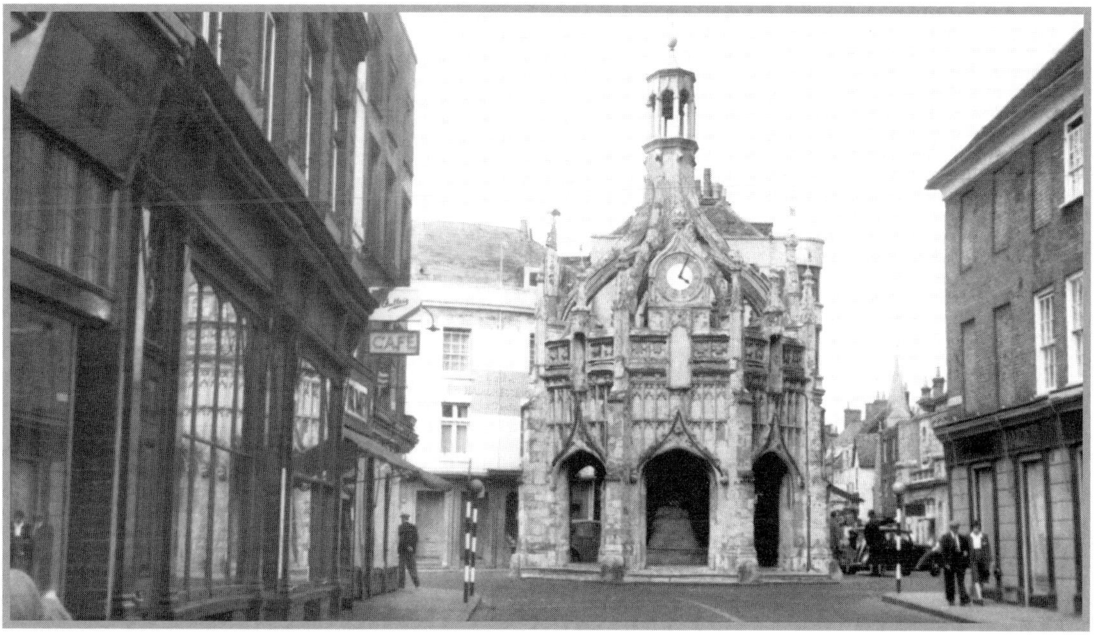

Market Cross c1955 C84010
At the end of South Street, the corner building on the left was replaced in the 1960s by the present Russell and Bromley shoeshop; fortunately, the one on the right with its 1709 date plaque was not replaced. Beyond, in North Street, Nash's Market House of 1807 and the set back upper storey of 1900 can be glimpsed.

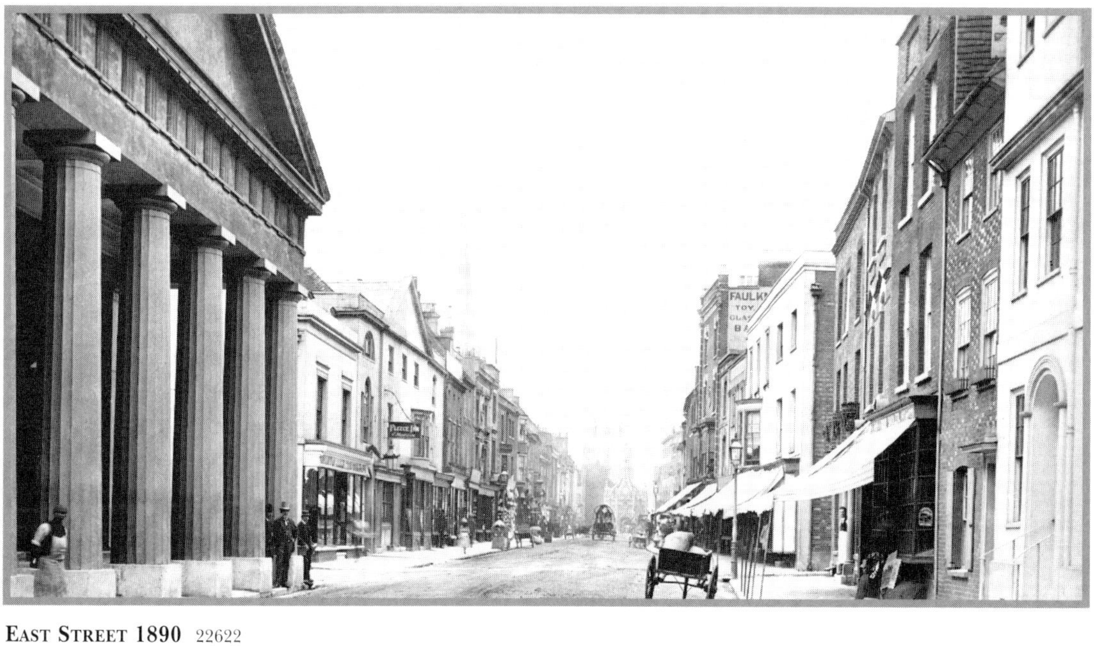

East Street 1890 22622
The splendid and monumental Corn Exchange of 1832, with its six giant fluted Greek Doric columns and towering pediment, later became a cinema; now, its temple-like facade houses the shrine of the hamburger as a McDonalds restaurant. The scale of the building reflects the importance of corn to the city's early 19th-century prosperity.

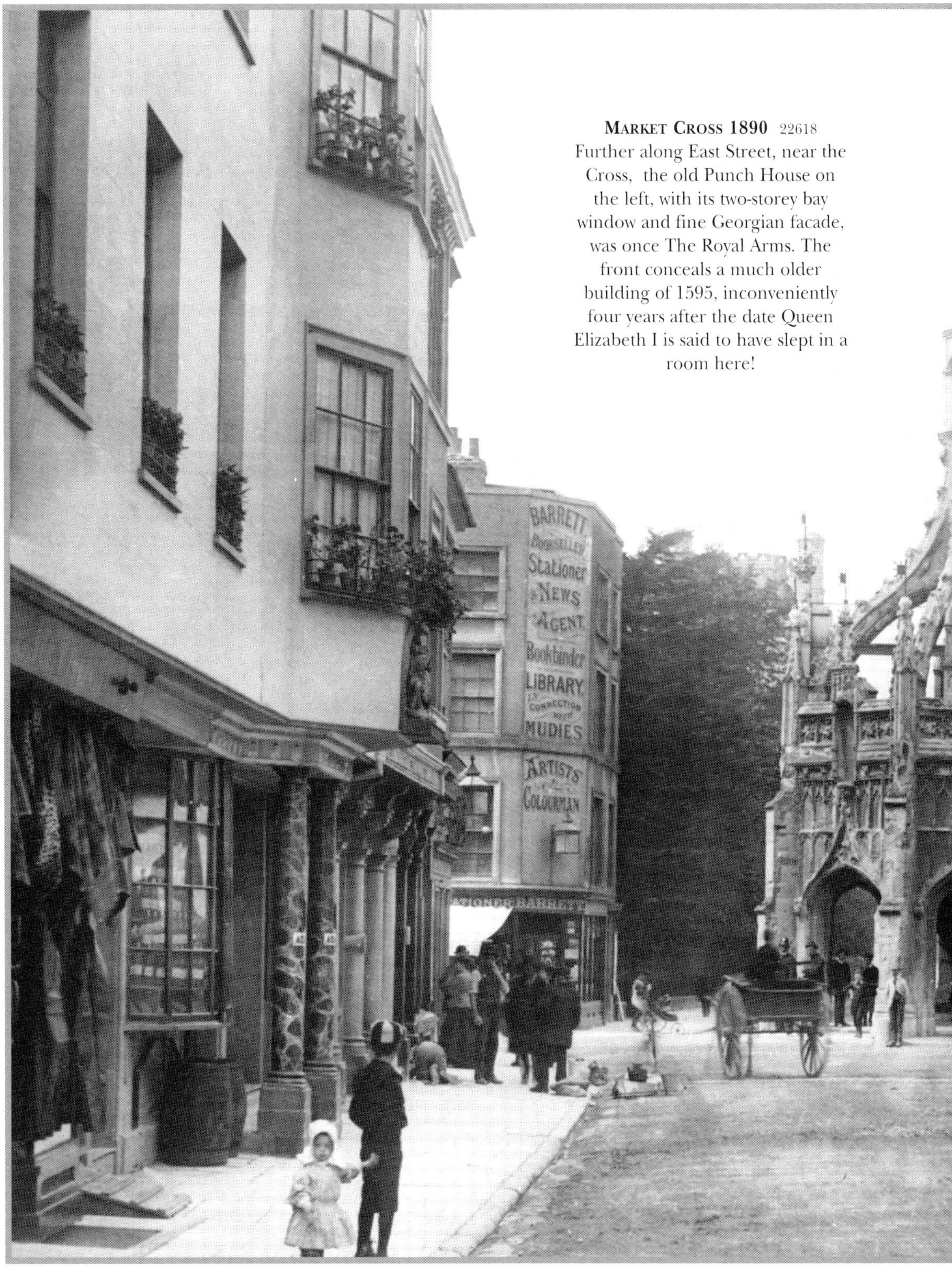

MARKET CROSS 1890 22618
Further along East Street, near the Cross, the old Punch House on the left, with its two-storey bay window and fine Georgian facade, was once The Royal Arms. The front conceals a much older building of 1595, inconveniently four years after the date Queen Elizabeth I is said to have slept in a room here!

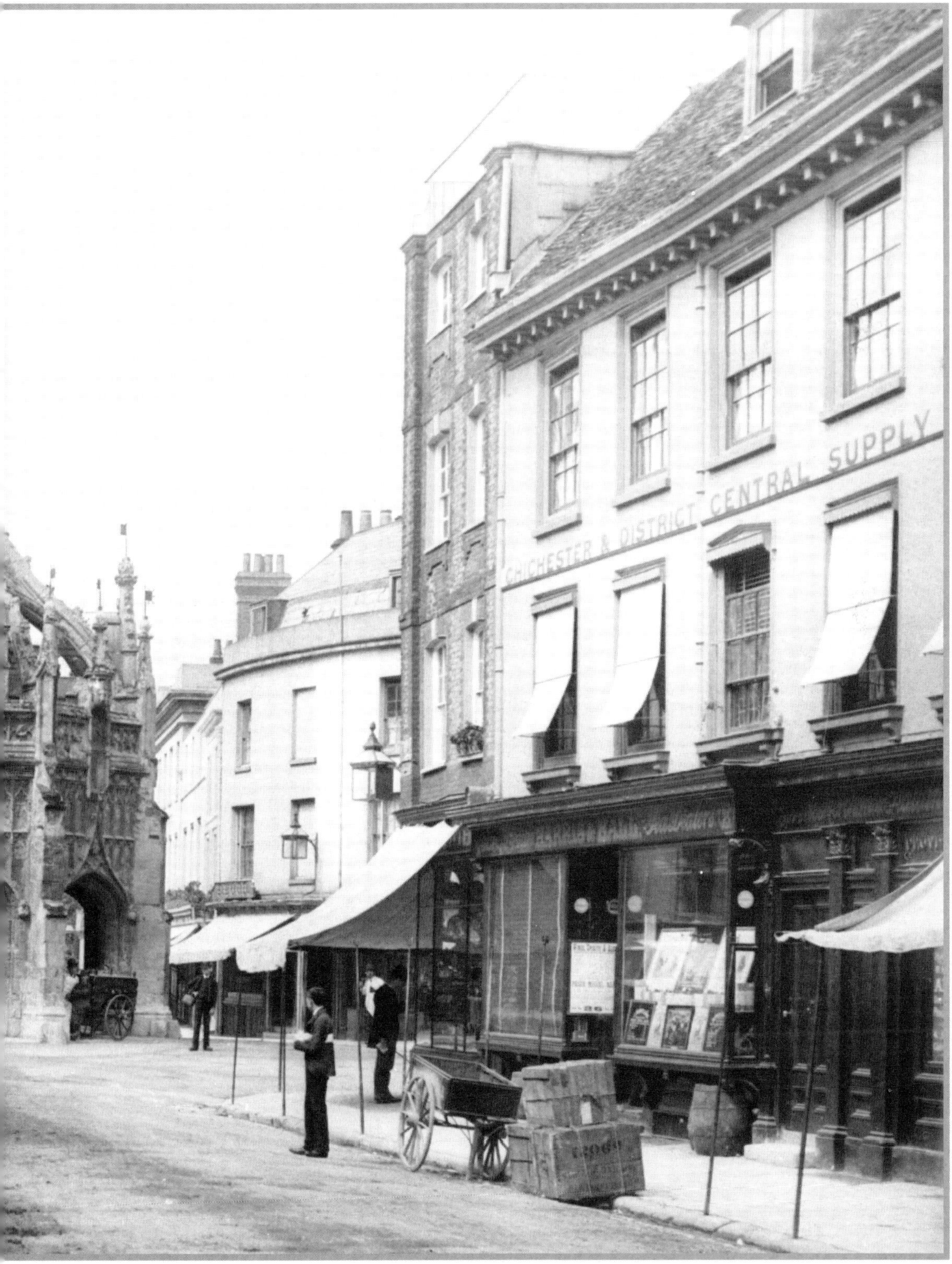
CHICHESTER & DISTRICT CENTRAL SUPPLY

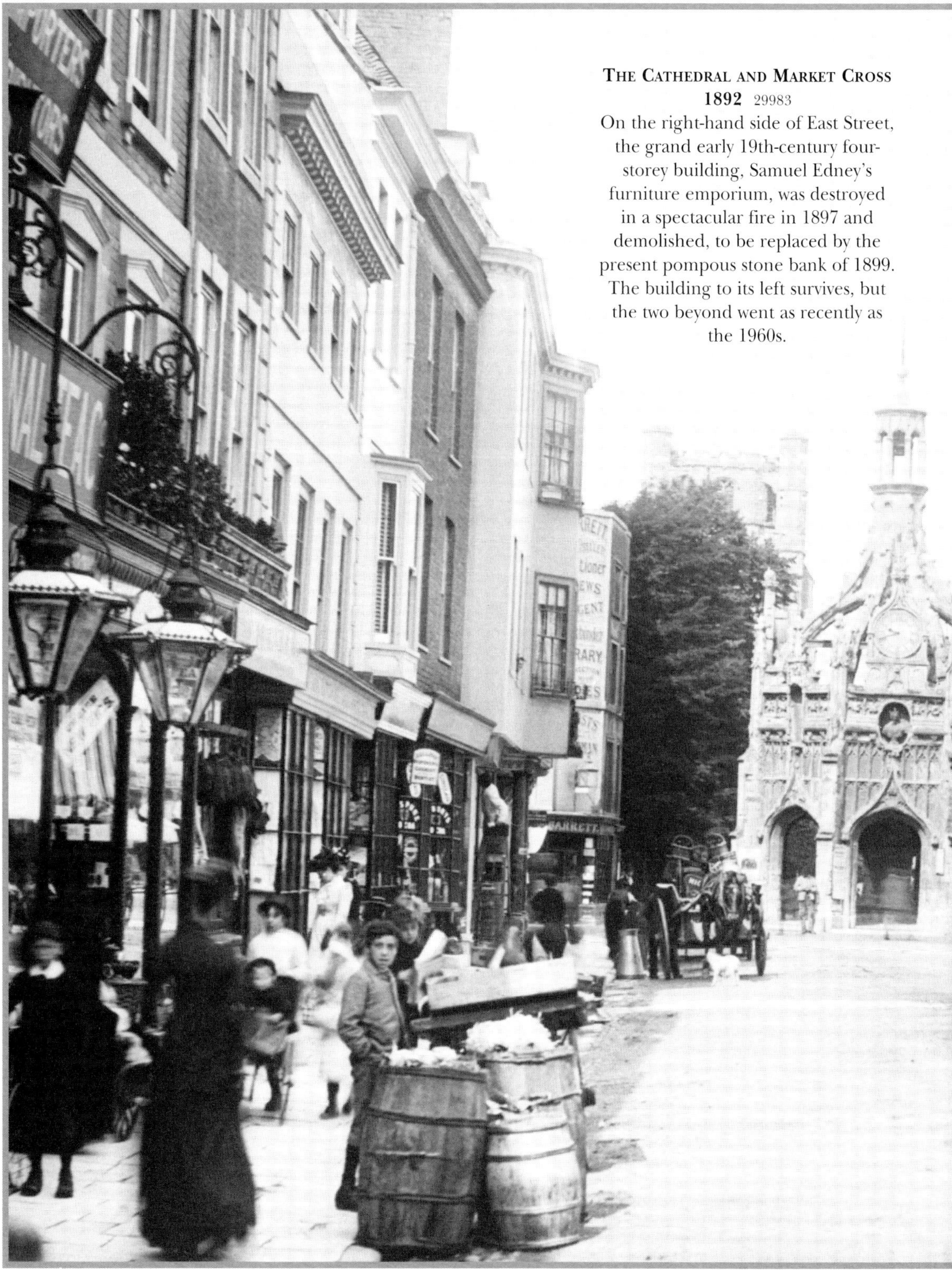

THE CATHEDRAL AND MARKET CROSS 1892 29983

On the right-hand side of East Street, the grand early 19th-century four-storey building, Samuel Edney's furniture emporium, was destroyed in a spectacular fire in 1897 and demolished, to be replaced by the present pompous stone bank of 1899. The building to its left survives, but the two beyond went as recently as the 1960s.

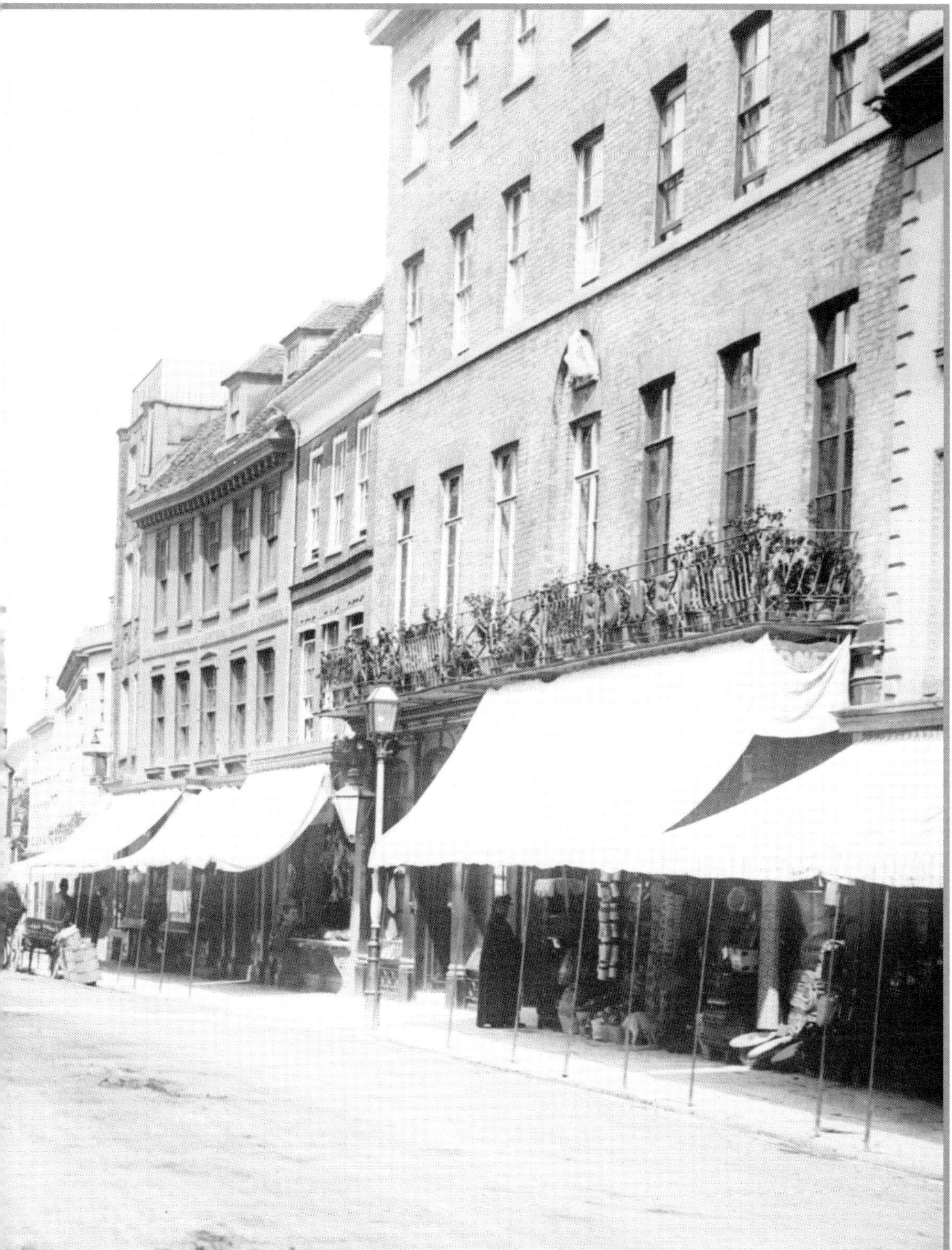

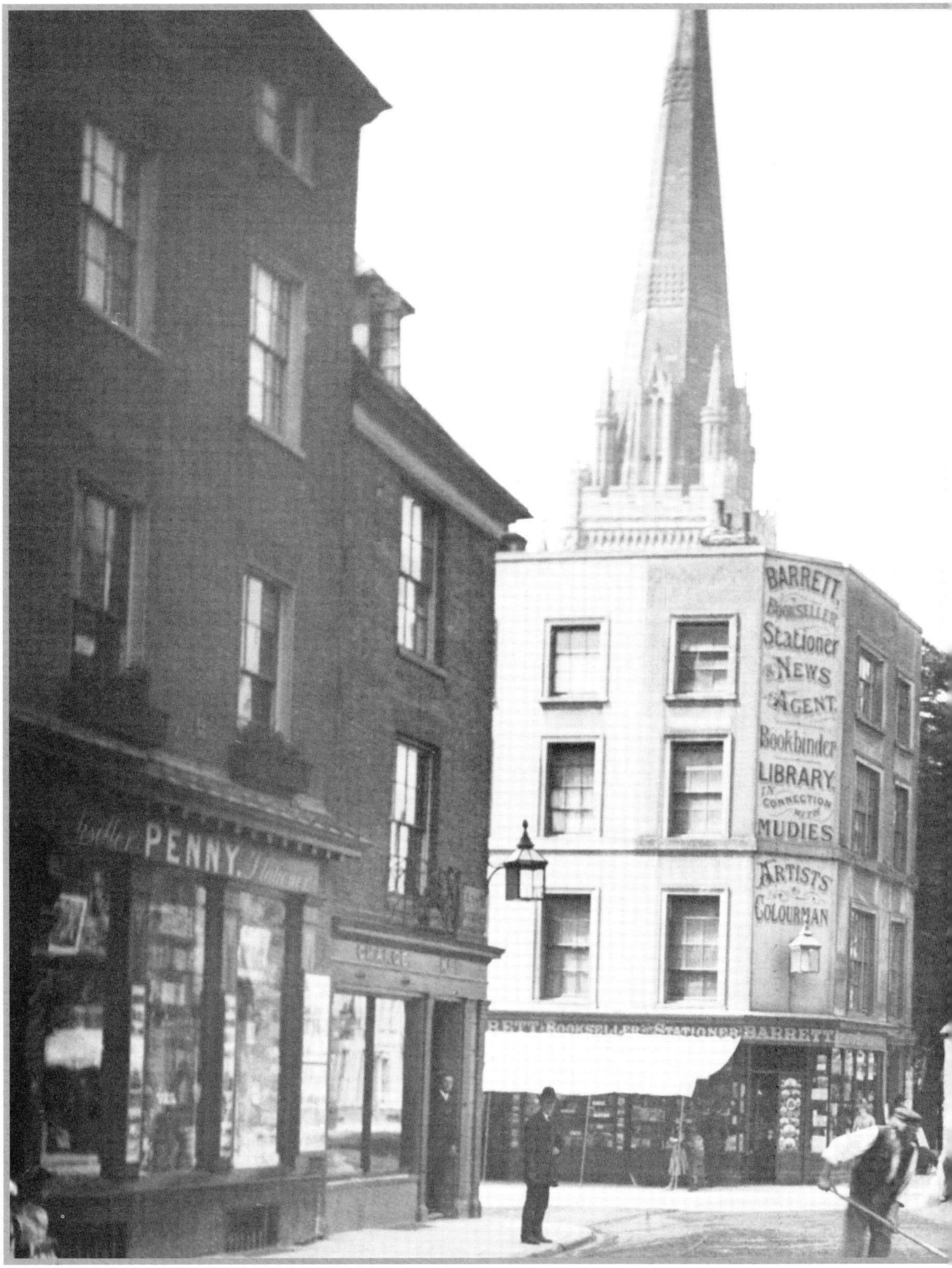
PENNY
BARRETT
Stationer
NEWS
AGENT
Bookbinder
LIBRARY
IN CONNECTION WITH
MUDIES
ARTISTS'
COLOURMAN
BARRETT

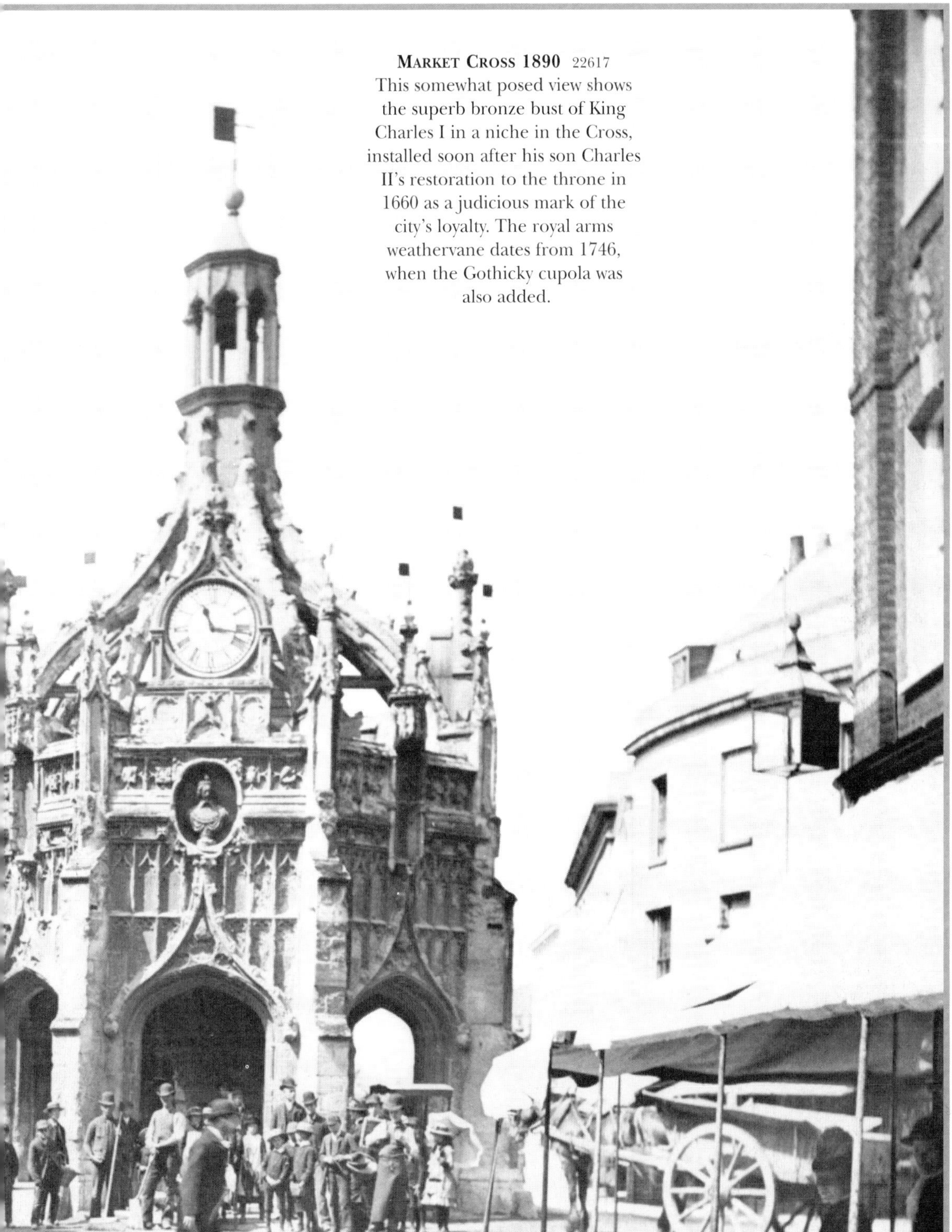

MARKET CROSS 1890 22617
This somewhat posed view shows the superb bronze bust of King Charles I in a niche in the Cross, installed soon after his son Charles II's restoration to the throne in 1660 as a judicious mark of the city's loyalty. The royal arms weathervane dates from 1746, when the Gothicky cupola was also added.

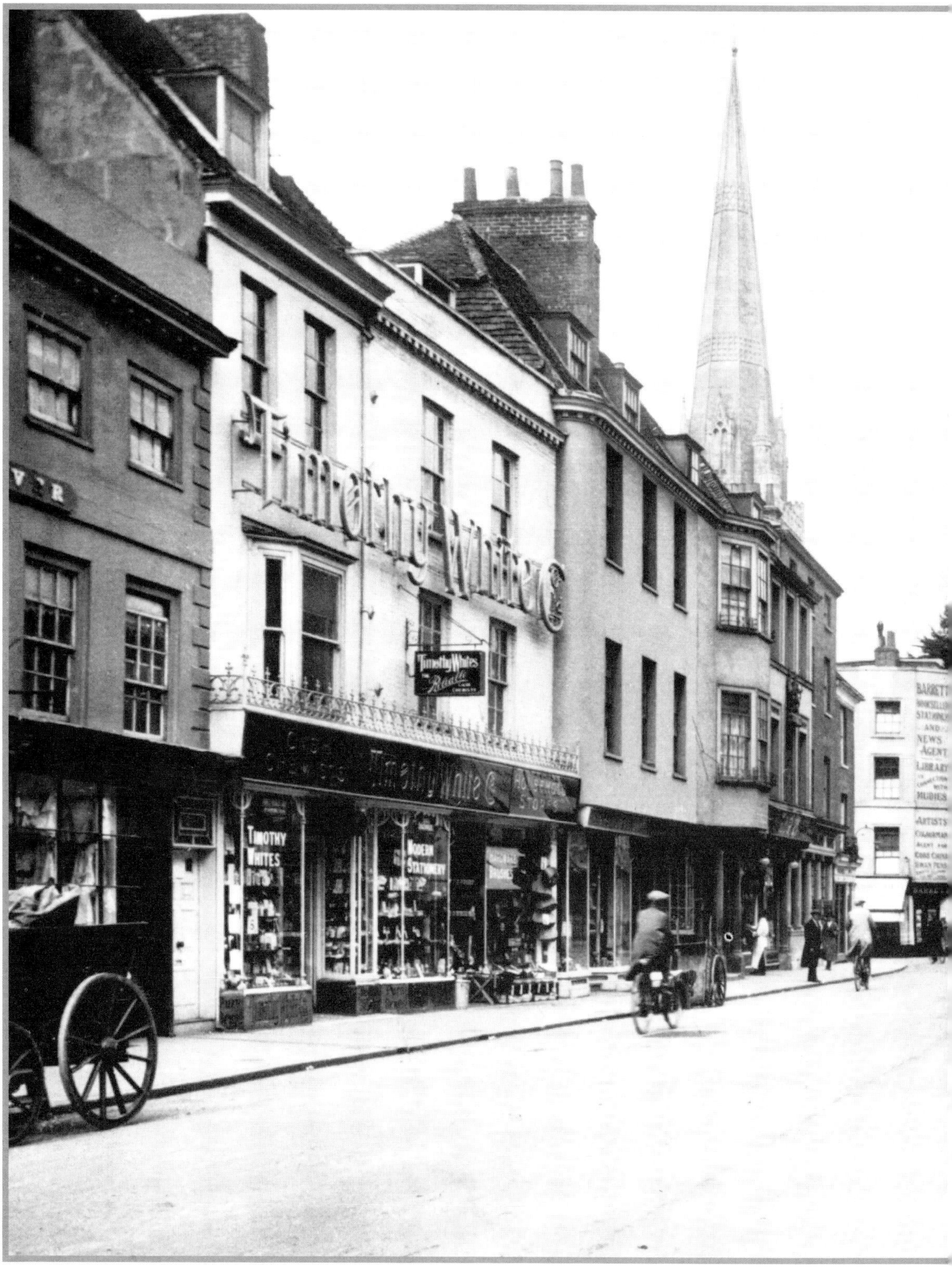
Timothy Whites
TIMOTHY WHITES
MODERN STATIONERY

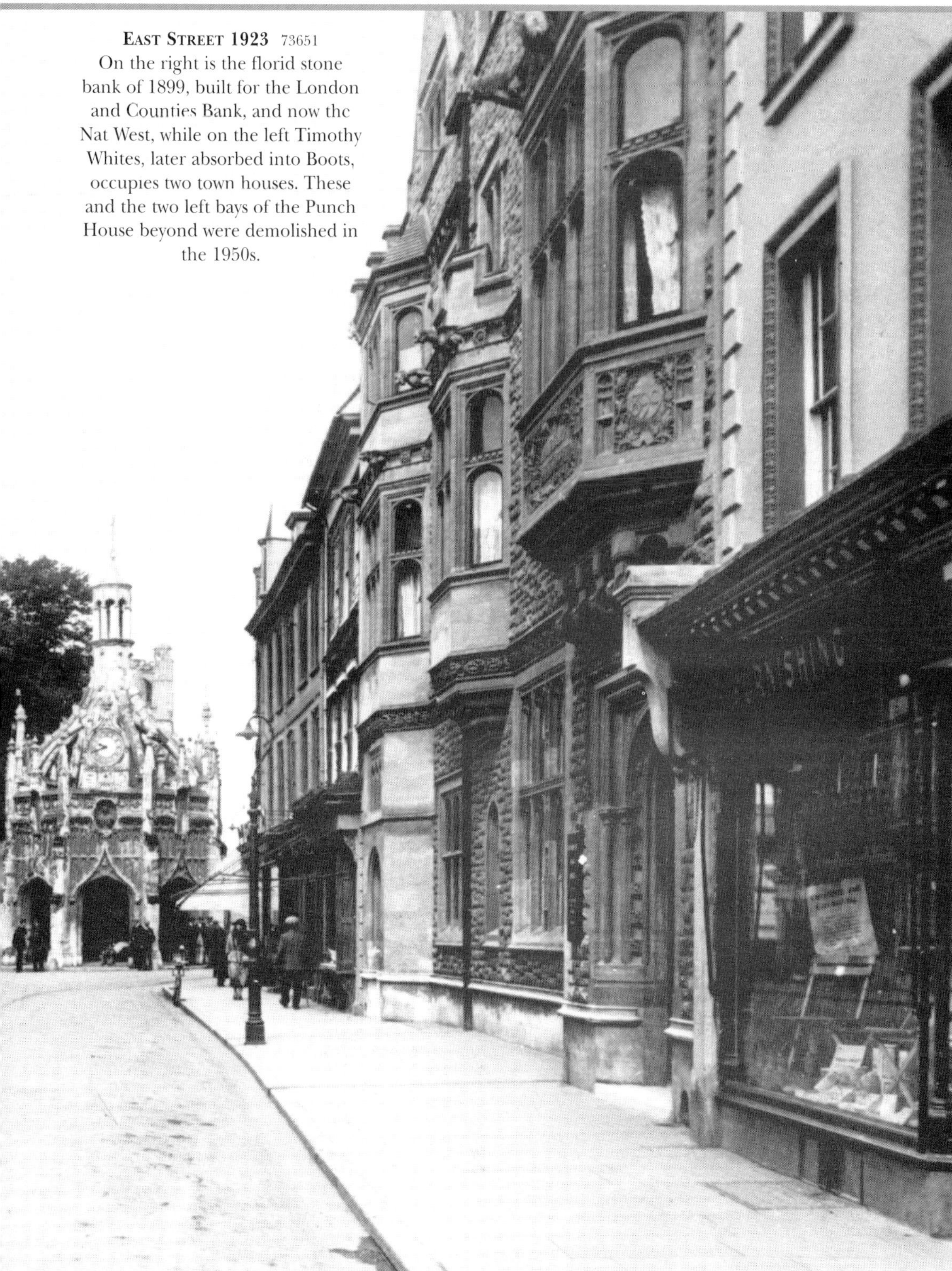

EAST STREET 1923 73651
On the right is the florid stone bank of 1899, built for the London and Counties Bank, and now the Nat West, while on the left Timothy Whites, later absorbed into Boots, occupies two town houses. These and the two left bays of the Punch House beyond were demolished in the 1950s.

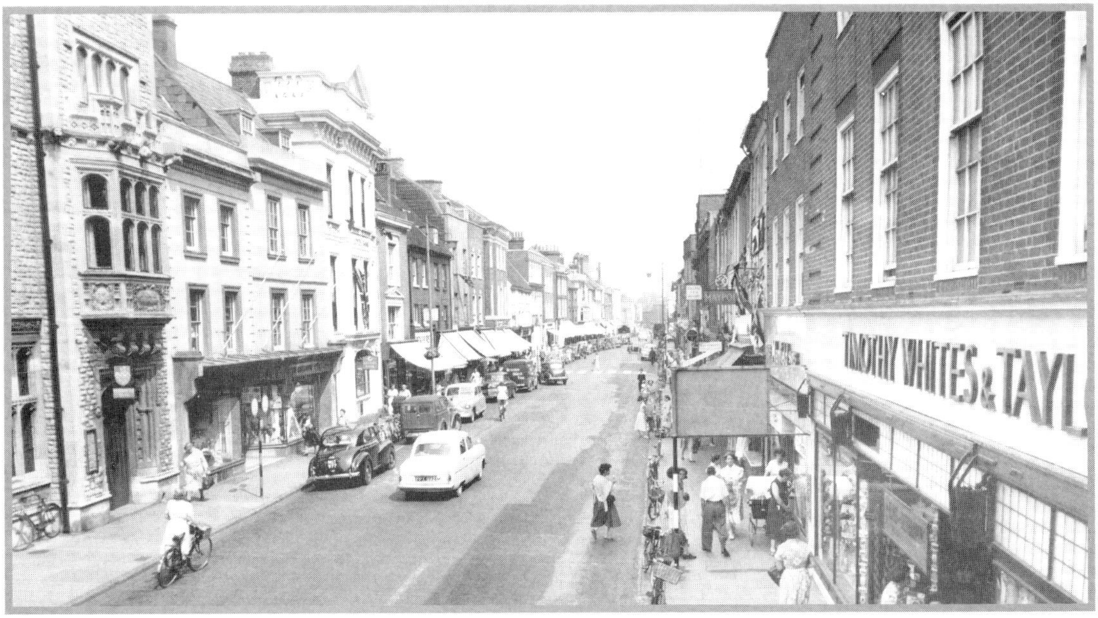

EAST STREET c1960 C84048

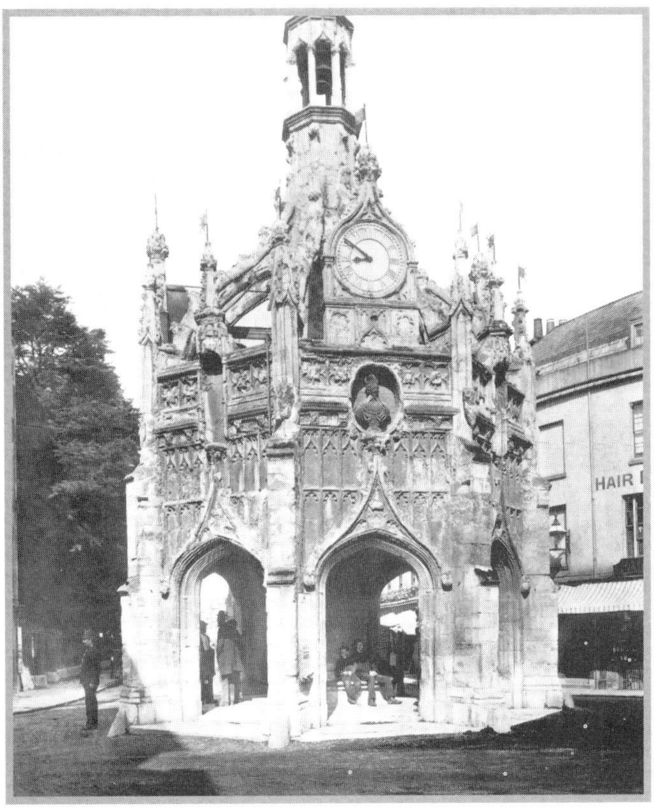

MARKET CROSS 1898 42676

EAST STREET c1960
This view looks east from the upper bay window of the Punch House. The replacement Timothy Whites and Taylors in pallid Neo-Georgian has appeared, now Boots, and the bank opposite, here the Westminster Bank, shows the curiously heavy Gothic style chosen for it in 1899 amidst the Georgian streets of Chichester.

MARKET CROSS 1898
A police constable waits for traffic or trouble while citizens, young and old, shelter from the sun beneath Bishop Storey's medieval Cross. The clocks which face down each of the main streets of the city were added in 1746, complete with stone ogee-arched Gothic-style surrounds. From 1809 until 1872 the Cross was surrounded by railings.

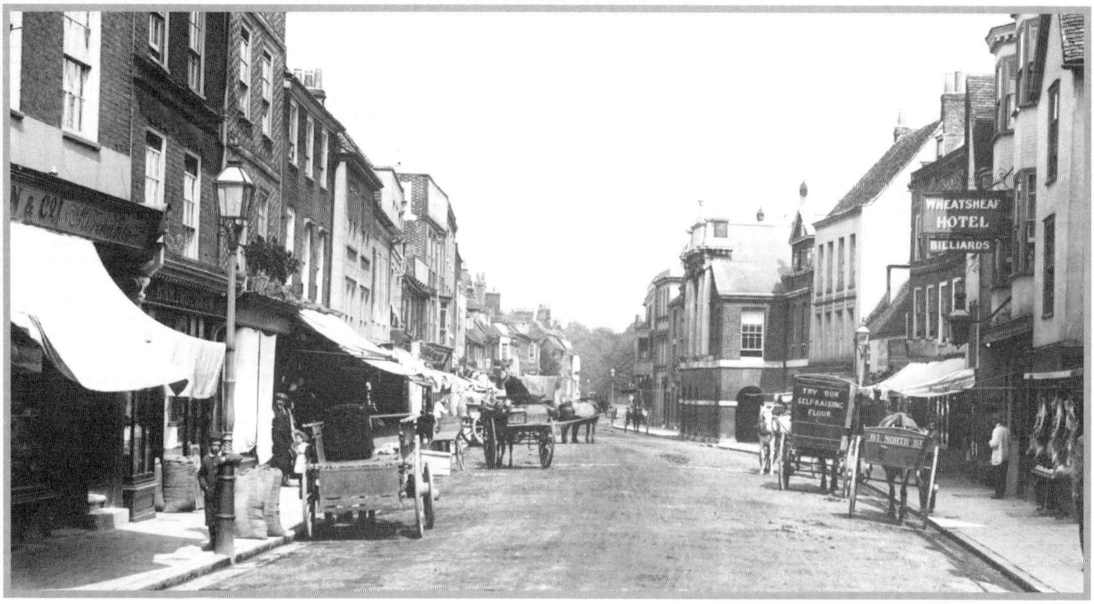

North Street 1898 42677
From this viewpoint there has since been much rebuilding from the 1940s to the 1970s, mostly not for the better, while the street is now pedestrianised. The column-fronted building built over the pavement on the right is the Council House of 1731, designed in a cheery provincial version of the then fashionable Palladian style by Roger Morris.

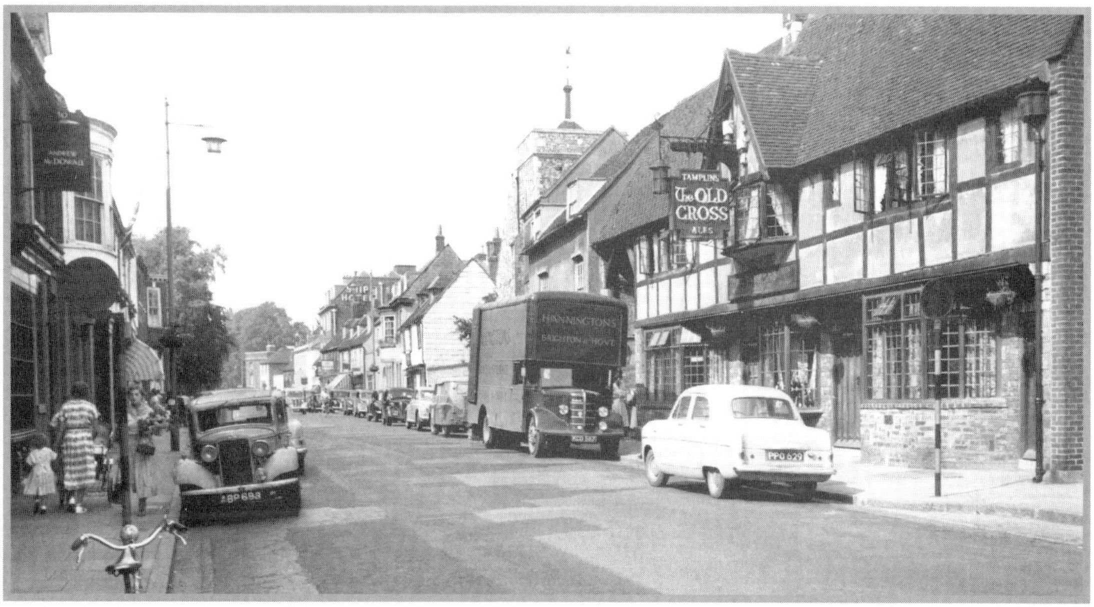

North Street c1955 C84070
Further north, the street has some fine Georgian town houses distinguished by central bay and oriel windows, including Purchase and Sons on the left, wine merchants here since 1780. Beyond the mock timber-framed 1920s Old Cross inn is the church of St Peter the Less, which was demolished in 1957 and replaced in the 1960s by a horrid block of flats.

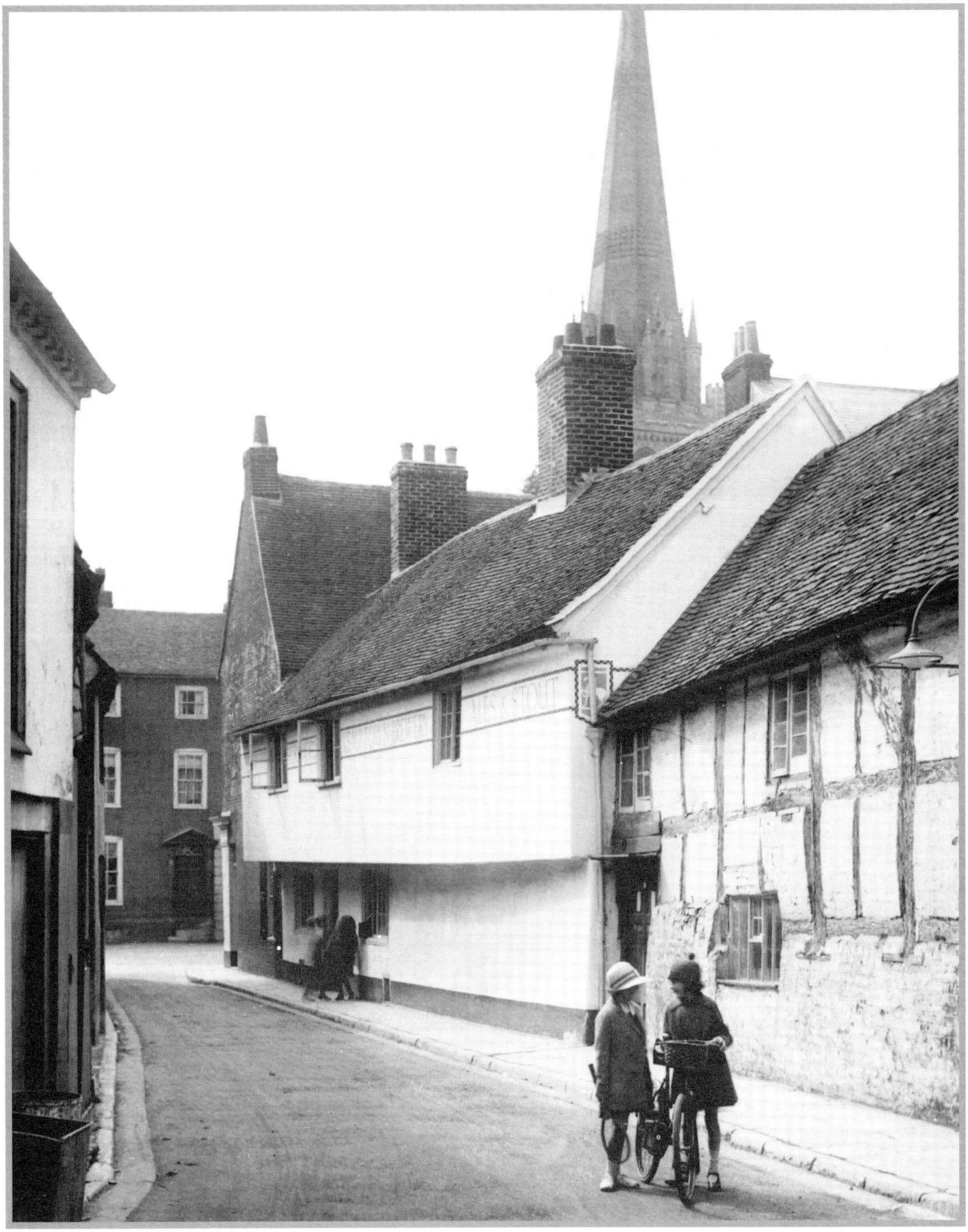

WEST PALLANT 1923 73657
This view along West Pallant looking towards South Street gives a good flavour of the city's winding lanes, where medieval streets developed more informally away from the straight main Roman through roads. The jettied and plastered building is part of the White Horse and survives, much trimmer now, but the timber-framed one attached does not.

The City Walls c1955
Chichester is a walled city, receiving its first stone walls under the Romans in about 200 AD. Their plan is roughly that of an eleven sided polygon, and there were fortified gateways at the end of North, East, South and West streets, all now gone. This view is along the eastern walls, looking north towards Priory Road.

The Walls c1965
Much of the walls survive, albeit much rebuilt and refaced with wide 18th-century rampart walkways added. You can walk along these rampart walks in the northern half of the city and view the walls in the south-west quarter from across the playing fields. Only in the south-east quadrant is the wall substantially hidden or missing.

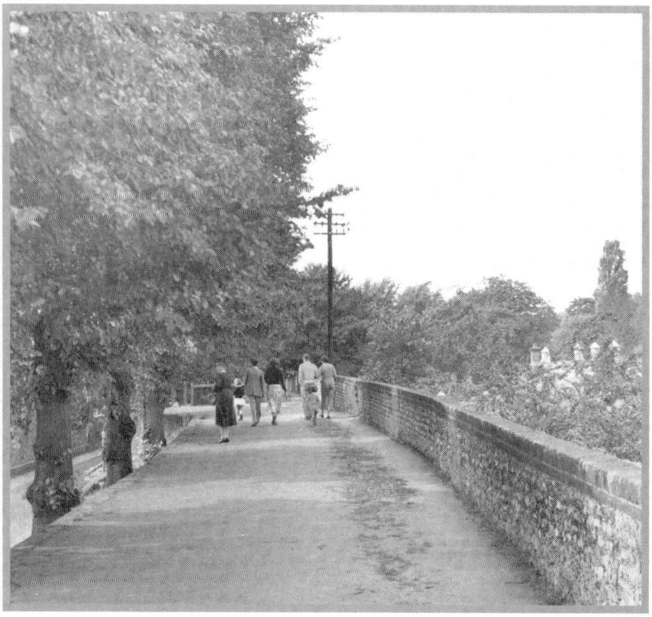

The City Walls c1955 C84029

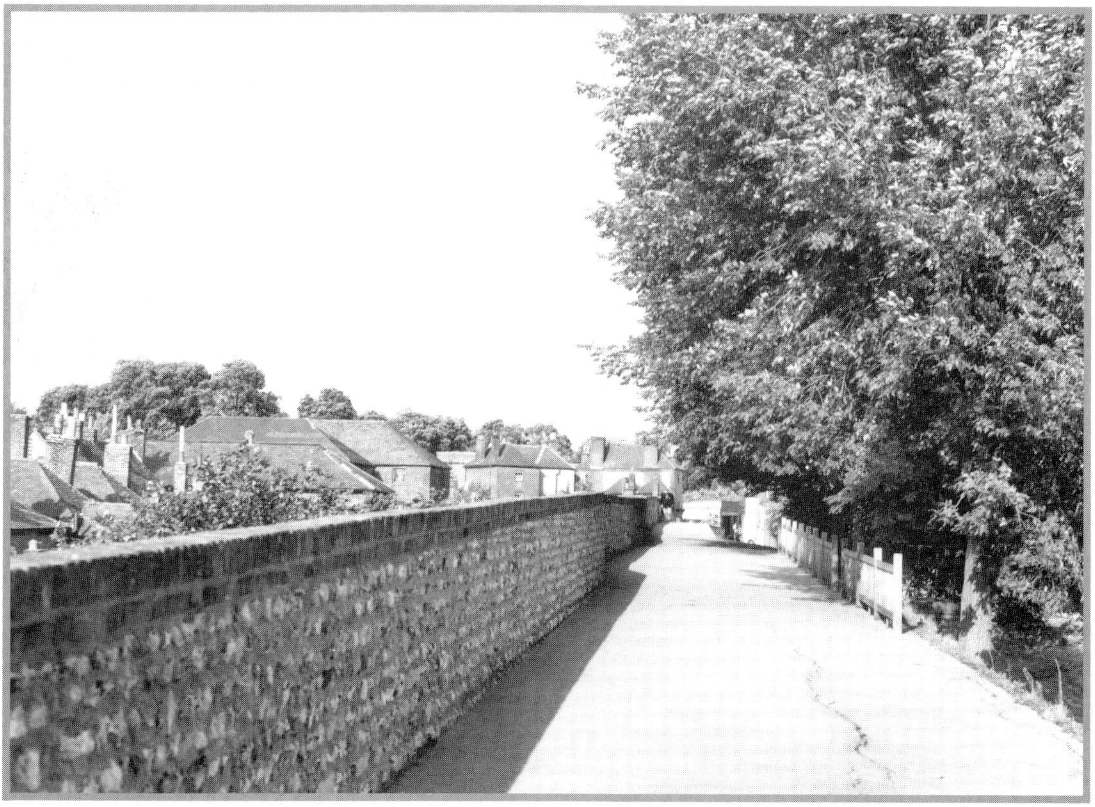

The Walls c1965 C84092

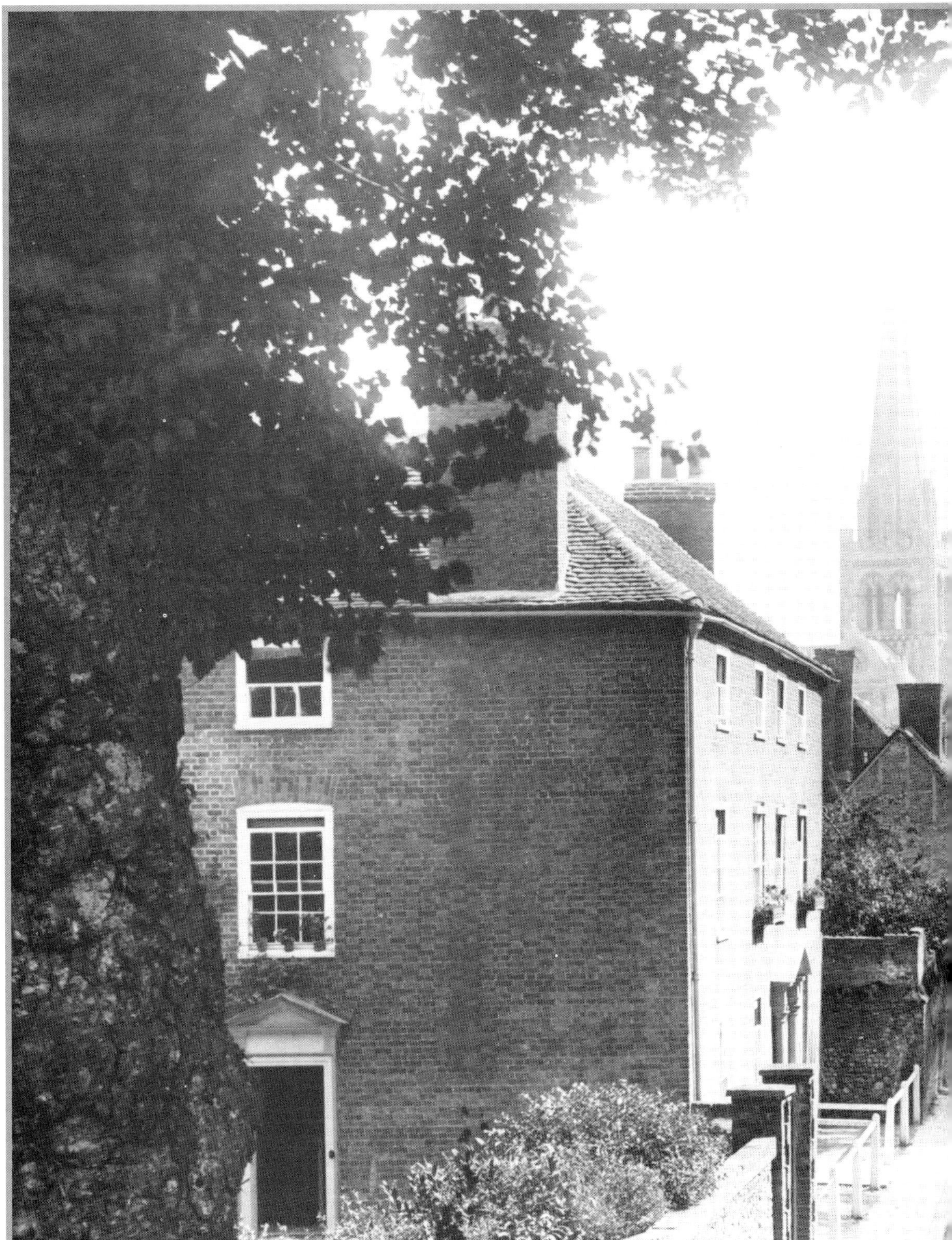

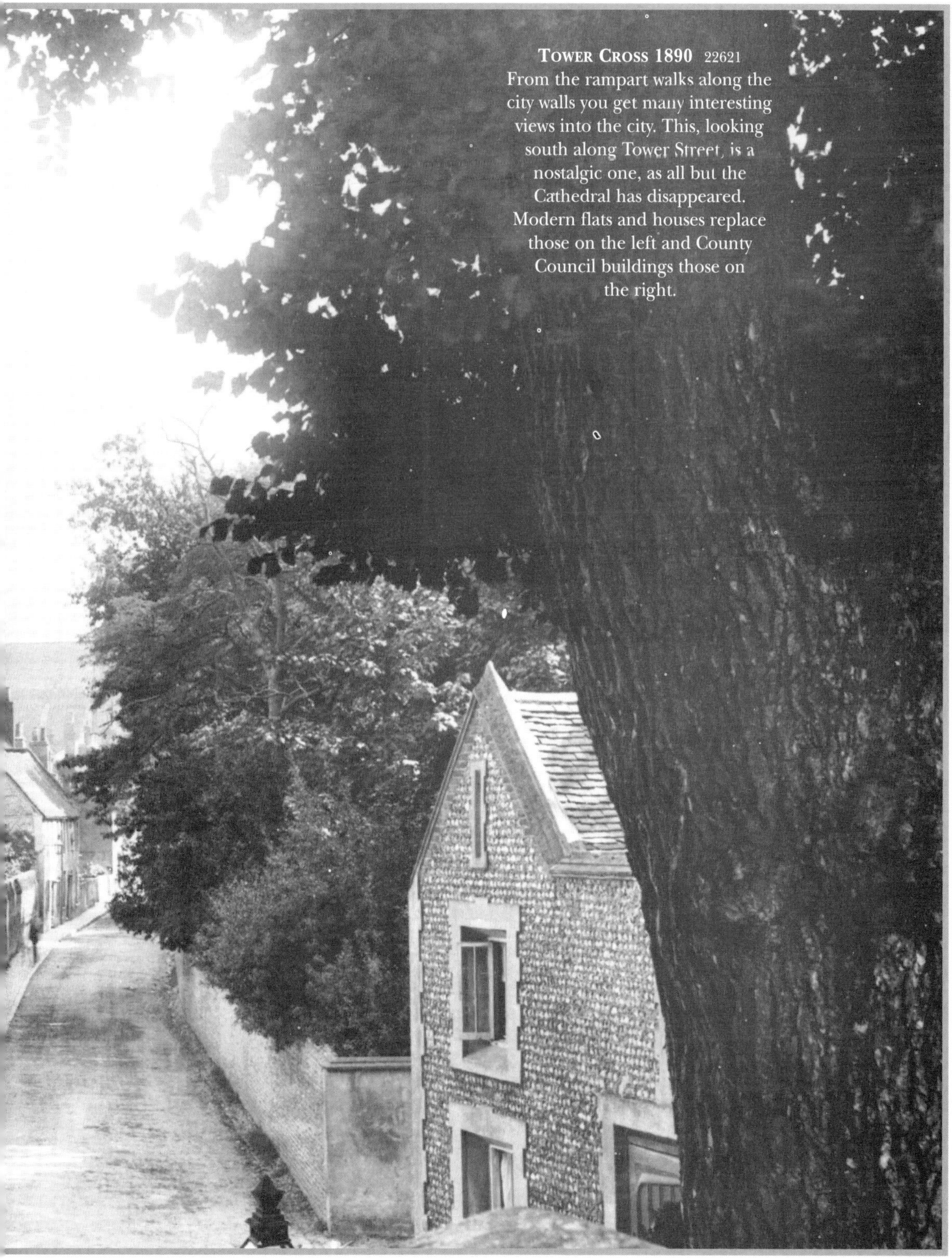

Tower Cross 1890 22621
From the rampart walks along the city walls you get many interesting views into the city. This, looking south along Tower Street, is a nostalgic one, as all but the Cathedral has disappeared. Modern flats and houses replace those on the left and County Council buildings those on the right.

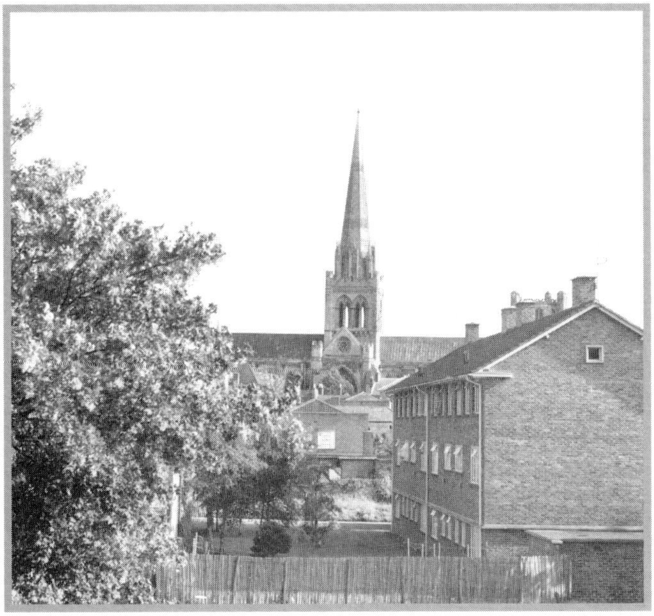

THE CATHEDRAL FROM THE WALLS c1960 C84091

THE CATHEDRAL FROM THE WALLS c1960
Tower Close, the houses on the right which front onto Tower Street, were built in the 1950s, and further 1970s ones in the foreground now block this view south from the north walls rampart walk. Much of the north-west quadrant of the city has been rebuilt, and it certainly suffered badly from bombing in World War II.

PRIORY PARK c1965
Priory Park, occupying much of the north part of the north-east quadrant, is the land granted to the Grey Friars in 1269. It included the site of the castle, demolished in 1217 and now a municipalised mound. This view looks south-west past the five great lancet windows of the Greyfriars church.

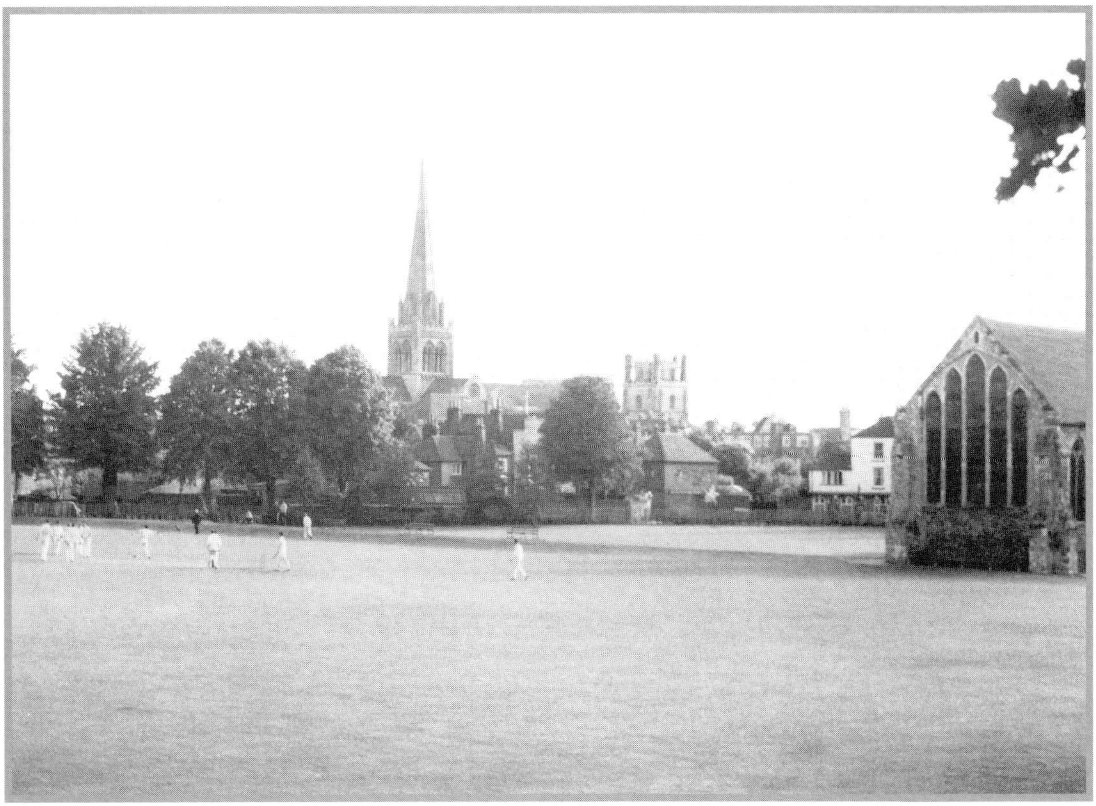

PRIORY PARK c1965 C84100

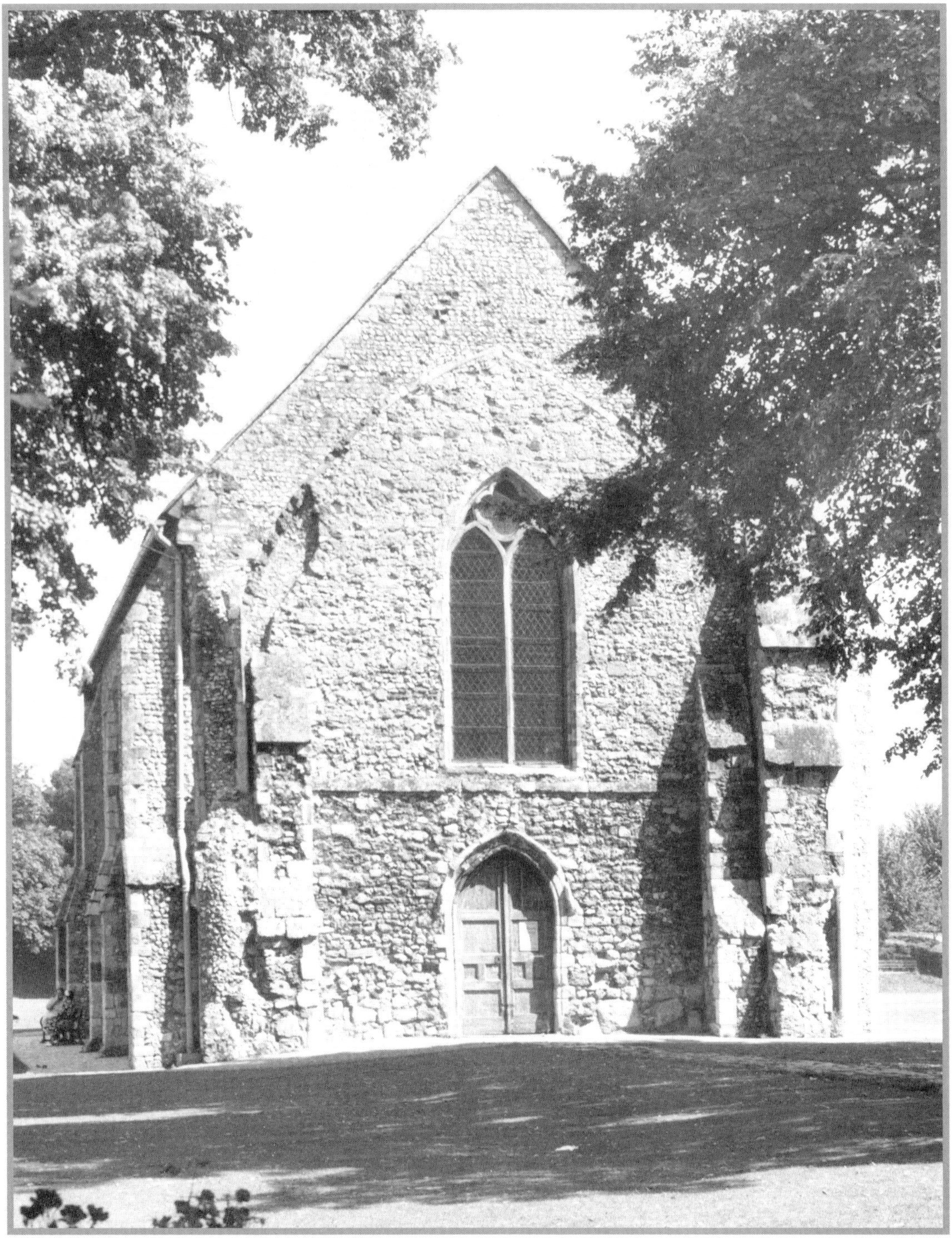

GREYFRIARS, PRIORY PARK c1955 C84036

Soon after 1269 the Grey Friars built this sumptuous church. They got no further than the choir, however, and the great arch seen in this view, intended to lead into a nave, was blocked by 1300. Dissolved by Henry VIII in 1538, the church had many subsequent uses, including as the city's guildhall and as an archaeological store.

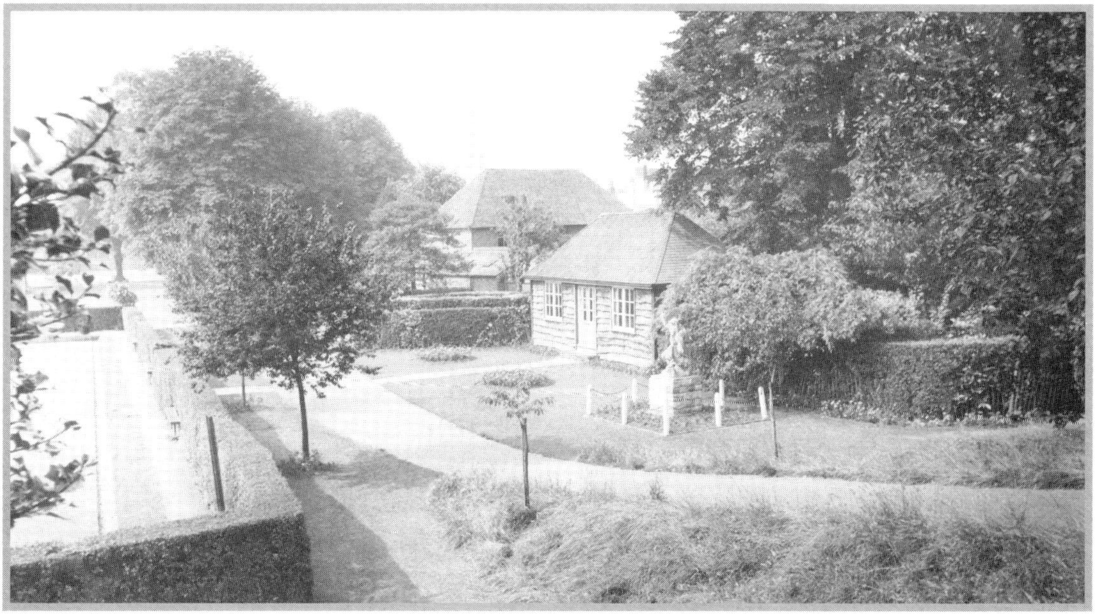

PRIORY PARK c1960 C84073

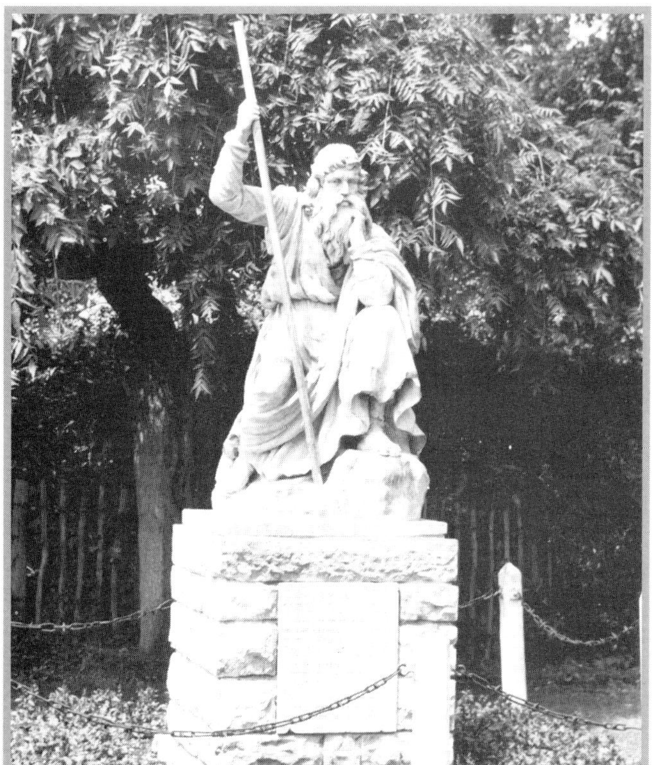

THE STATUE TO WILLIAM GUY, SURGEON c1960 C84085

PRIORY PARK c1960
On 30th September 1918, before World War I had ended, the Duke of Richmond and Gordon presented the park to the citizens 'as a war memorial and for public recreation'. This view looks south past the bowling green from the city wall, which forms the north and east park boundary.

THE STATUE TO WILLIAM GUY, SURGEON c1960
Near the bowling green is an 18th century statue of Moses striking the rock to bring forth water, which once stood on the conduit house at the public drinking supply fountain in South Street. Later it was in the cathedral vault of the surgeon William Guy, whose grandson presented it to Priory Park in 1873.

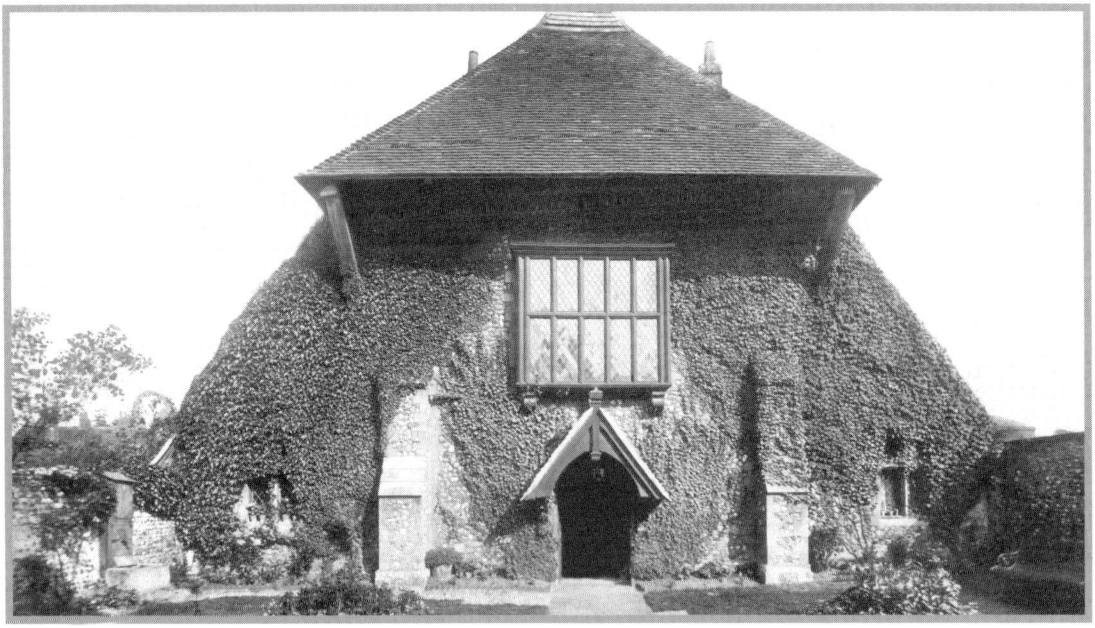

St Mary's Almshouses 1898 42682

St Mary's Almshouses 1898
This building is one of the most remarkable survivals in Europe: a virtually unchanged medieval hospital, its hall and chapel dating from the late 13th century. The sick-bay hall was divided into almshouses in the 17th century, which preserved the buildings intact. Through the gateway from St Martin's Square this west front immediately faces you.

The War Memorial 1923
In July 1921 this fine war memorial was unveiled in Eastgate Square, just beyond the city walls. Behind is The Unicorn, which was demolished in the 1950s to make way for the premises of the Chichester Observer; the war memorial itself was moved to Litten Gardens further east to avoid inconveniencing the motor car.

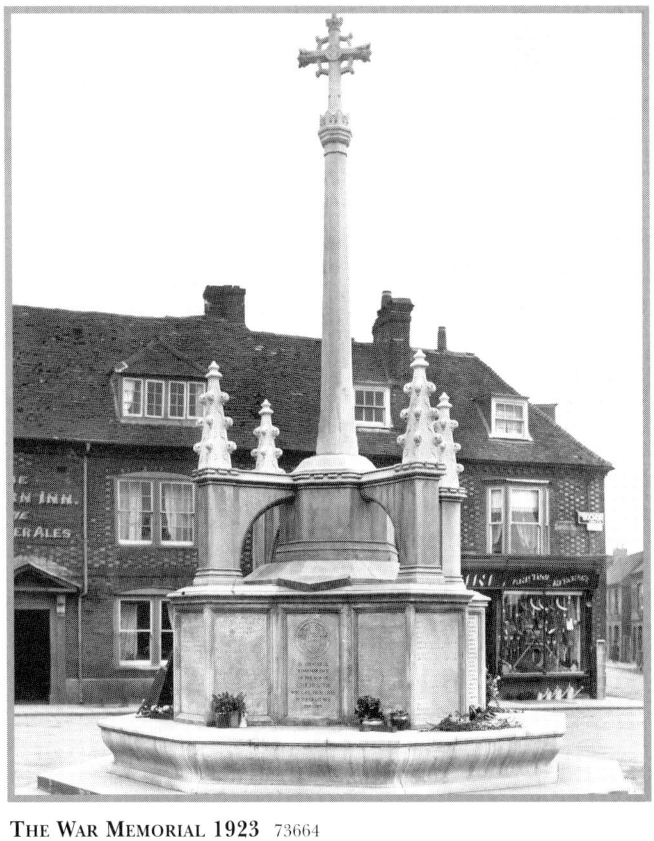

The War Memorial 1923 73664

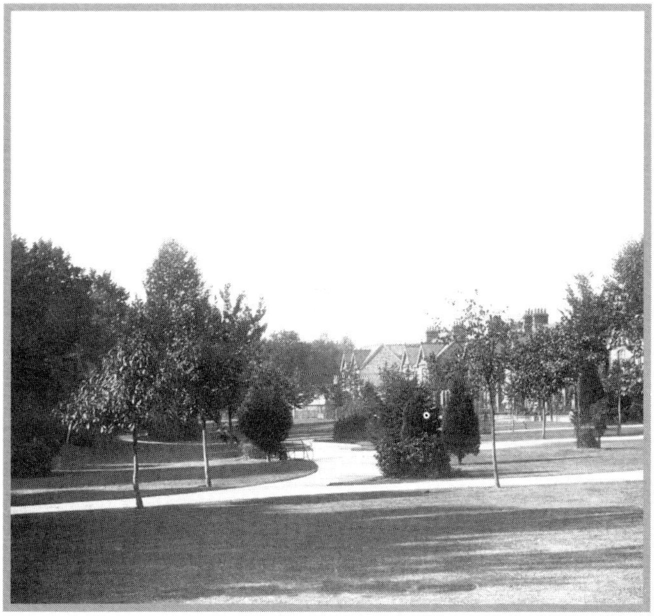

NEW PARK 1898 42683

NEW PARK 1898

As the city expanded in Victorian times beyond the walls to the east, the area between the New Park Road and the city walls was laid out as a public park to commemorate Queen Victoria's Golden Jubilee. In this view, taken within the shade of tall cedars, the trees on the left screen the city walls.

THE FESTIVAL THEATRE c1965

Chichester's world-renowned Festival Theatre is a thoroughly modern building designed by Powell and Moya. Opening in 1962, it was the brainchild of a former mayor, Leslie Evershed-Martin. Built amid the fine trees of Oaklands Park, which had been bought by the city in 1939, its first director was none other than Sir Laurence Olivier.

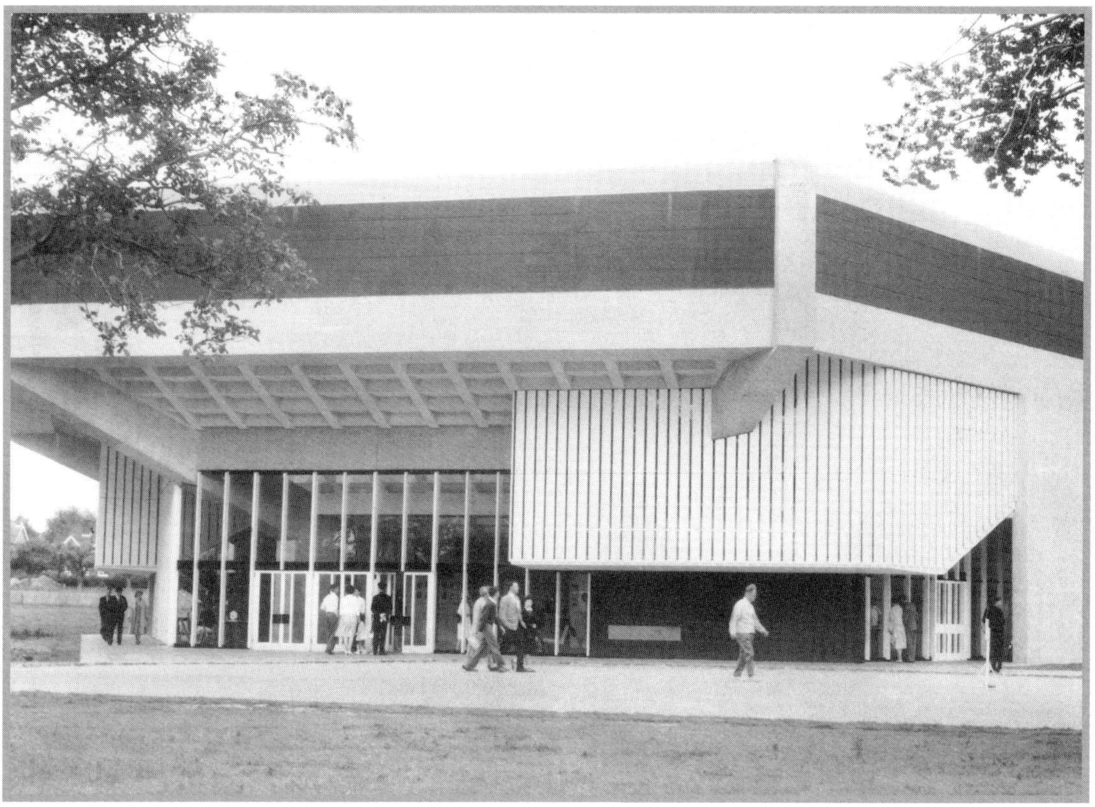

THE FESTIVAL THEATRE c1965 C84118

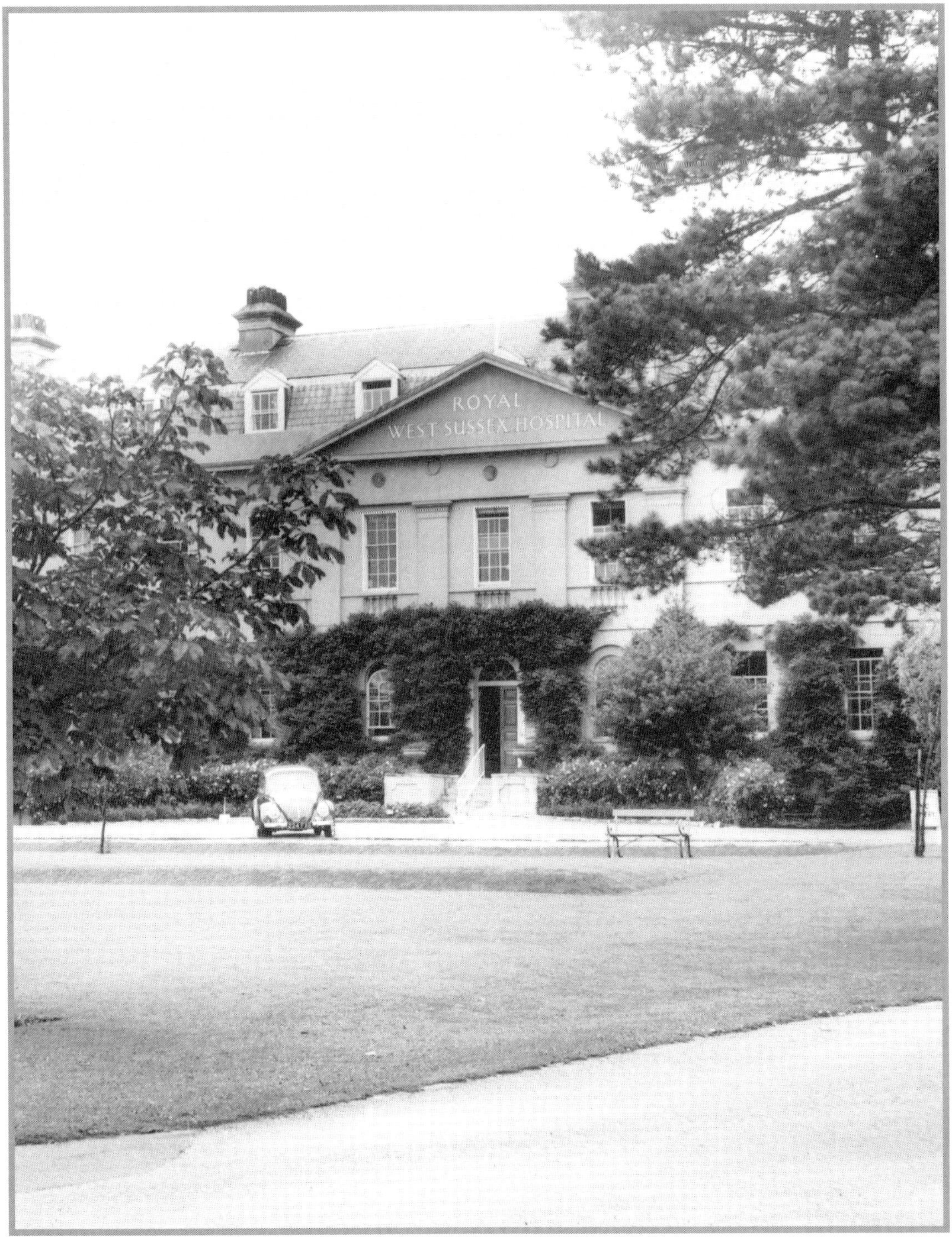

The Royal West Sussex Hospital c1965 C84139

The hospital closed recently. Its main block, a long stuccoed range of 1828 (largely reconstructed in 1913), with its central pediment seen here between the trees, is now converted to flats as part of King George Gardens, an estate of neo-Georgian houses which occupy the site of the other hospital buildings.

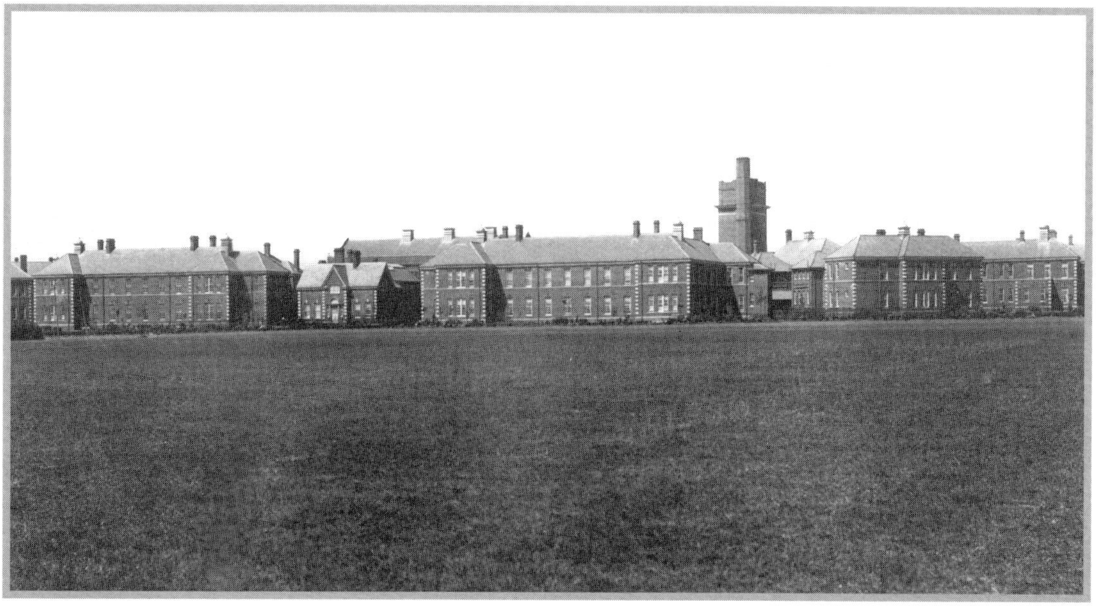

GRAYLINGWELL HOSPITAL 1898 42678
Now the headquarters of the Sussex Weald and Downs National Health Service Trust, this Victorian former county lunatic asylum is a truly awesome sprawl situated north-east of the walled city off College Lane, east of the barracks. Seen here from the south, across what are now playing fields softened by trees, the bleakness of the environment comes over well.

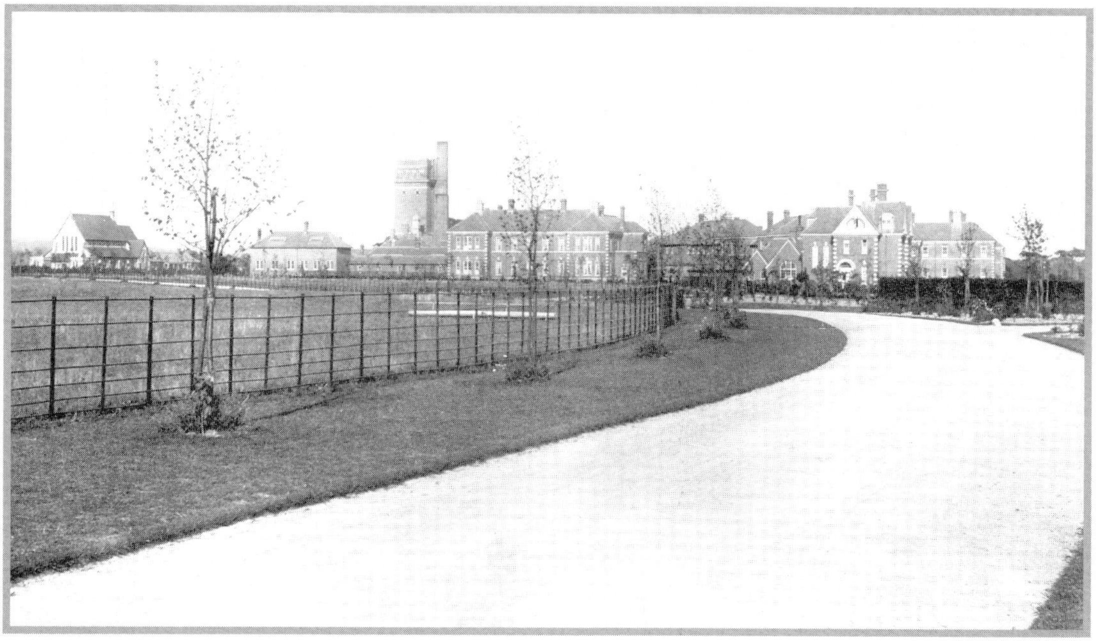

GRAYLINGWELL HOSPITAL ENTRANCE 1898 42679
In 1898 the park fence and tree planting was brand new; this view along the entrance drive from College Lane can no longer be seen, as these and many other trees have fully matured. Note the tall water tower which can be seen for miles around, the only rival from the Downs for the cathedral spire.

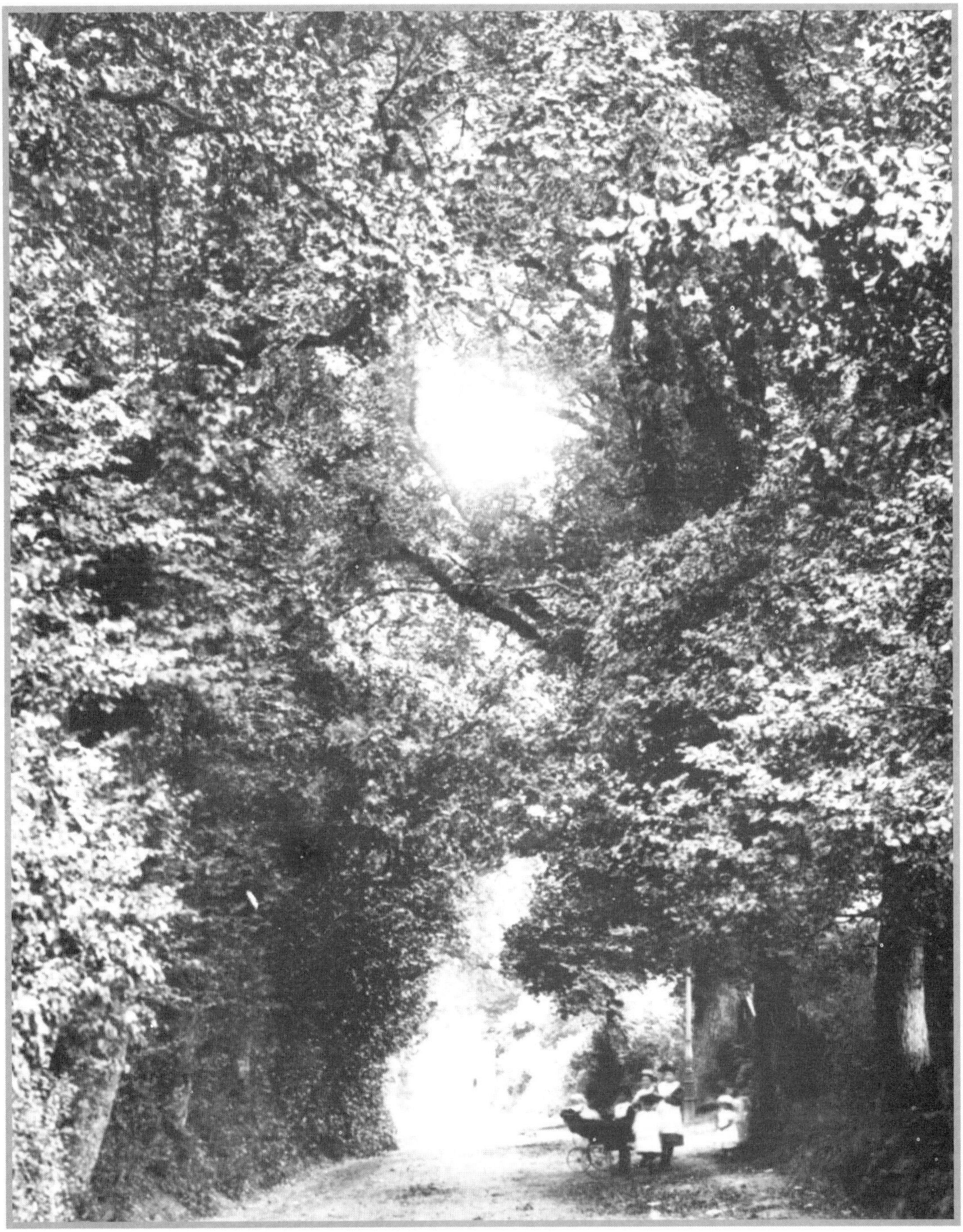

LOVE LANE 1898 42685

The children posing with their perambulator in this tree-lined lane near Chichester would be unwise to do so now, for the road (renamed College Lane when the Bishop Otter Memorial College was founded) is now a busy one. The Bishop Otter Memorial College has itself been renamed and is now the University College of Chichester.

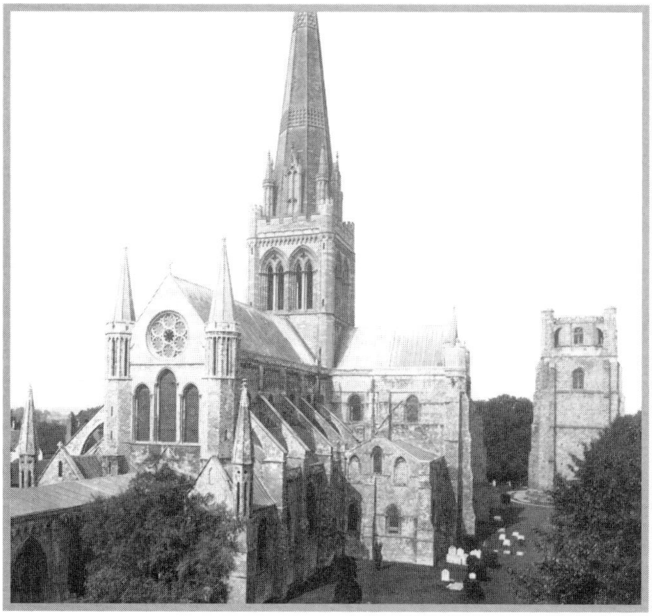

THE CATHEDRAL, FROM NORTH EAST 1892 29984

THE CATHEDRAL
from North East 1892
The Cathedral, and especially its 277 ft high spire, dominate the town and the countryside for miles around, as indeed it should, for it is the mother church of Sussex. The cathedral was started about 1091 by Bishop Ralph Luffa, and in the main remains a Norman building with later additions, including the spire.

THE OLD GATEWAY c1955
Our tour enters the cathedral close via the medieval gateway from South Street into Canon Lane, the rear of which is shown in this view. The shield bears the coat of arms of Edward More, the Archdeacon of Lewes in the late 1520s, which must date the building of the gate.

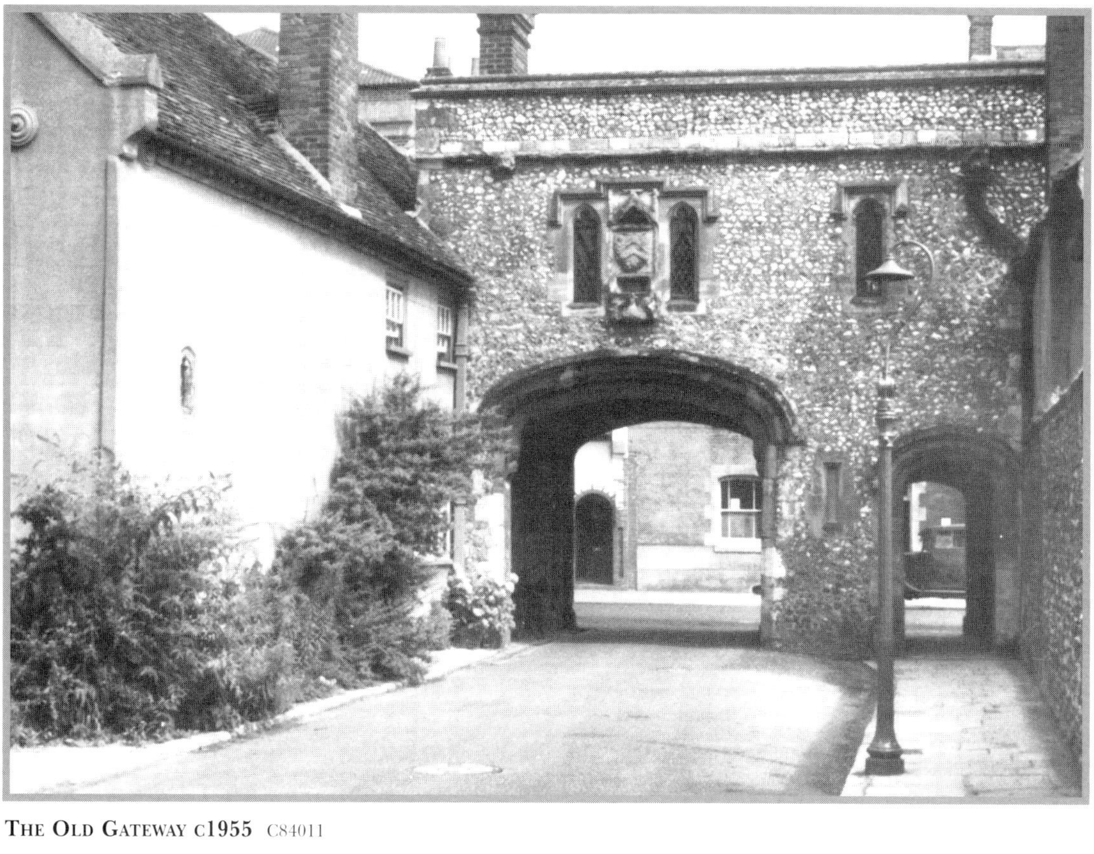

THE OLD GATEWAY c1955 C84011

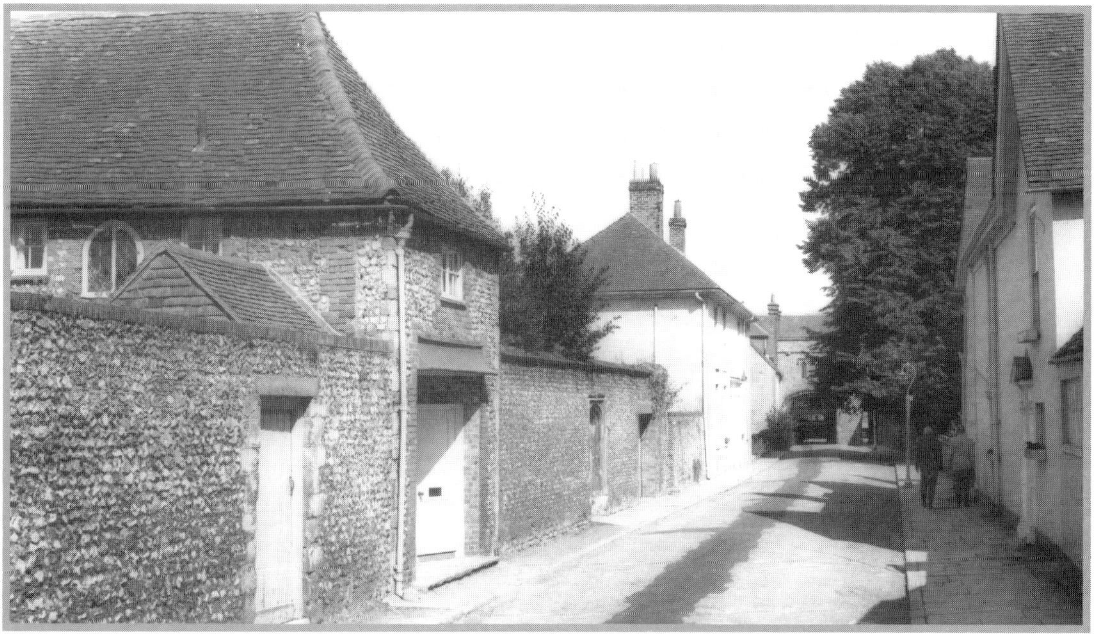

Canon Lane c1965 C84213
Canon Lane leads from the Bishop's Palace, behind the photographer to South Street seen in the distance. The Residentiary, a Georgian casing of a medieval house, is on the right and Blackman House is the painted building in the middle distance on the left.

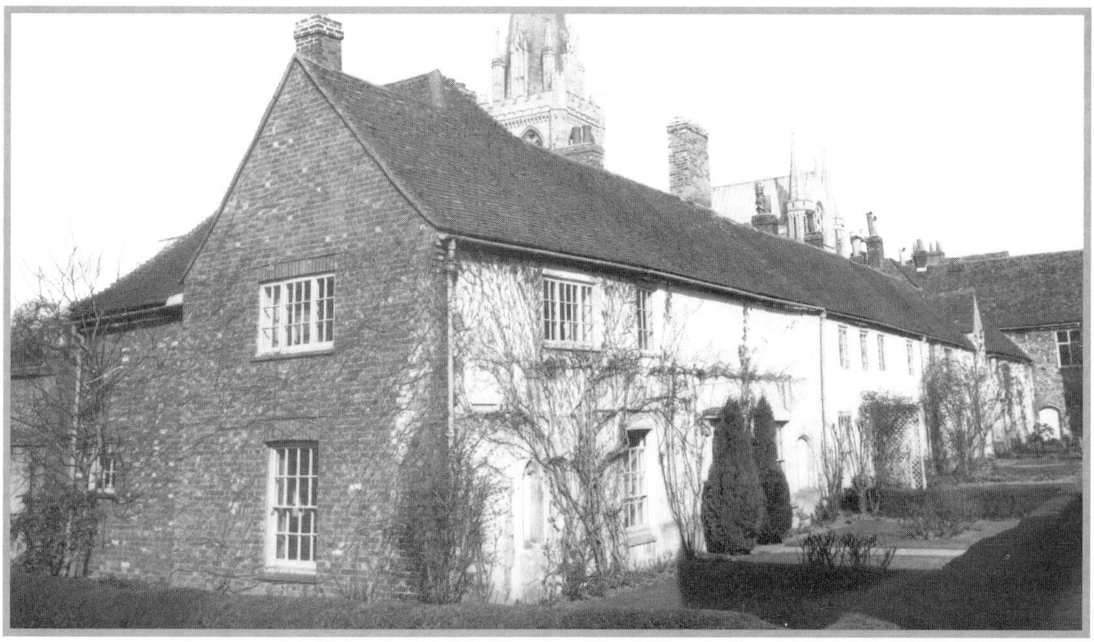

Vicars Close c1965 C84187
This view is of the west terrace of houses built for the Vicars Choral of the cathedral and dating from the 15th century, seen from Canon Lane. Those on the east side of the path, out of view to the right, were converted into shops in 1825 and given fronts to South Street.

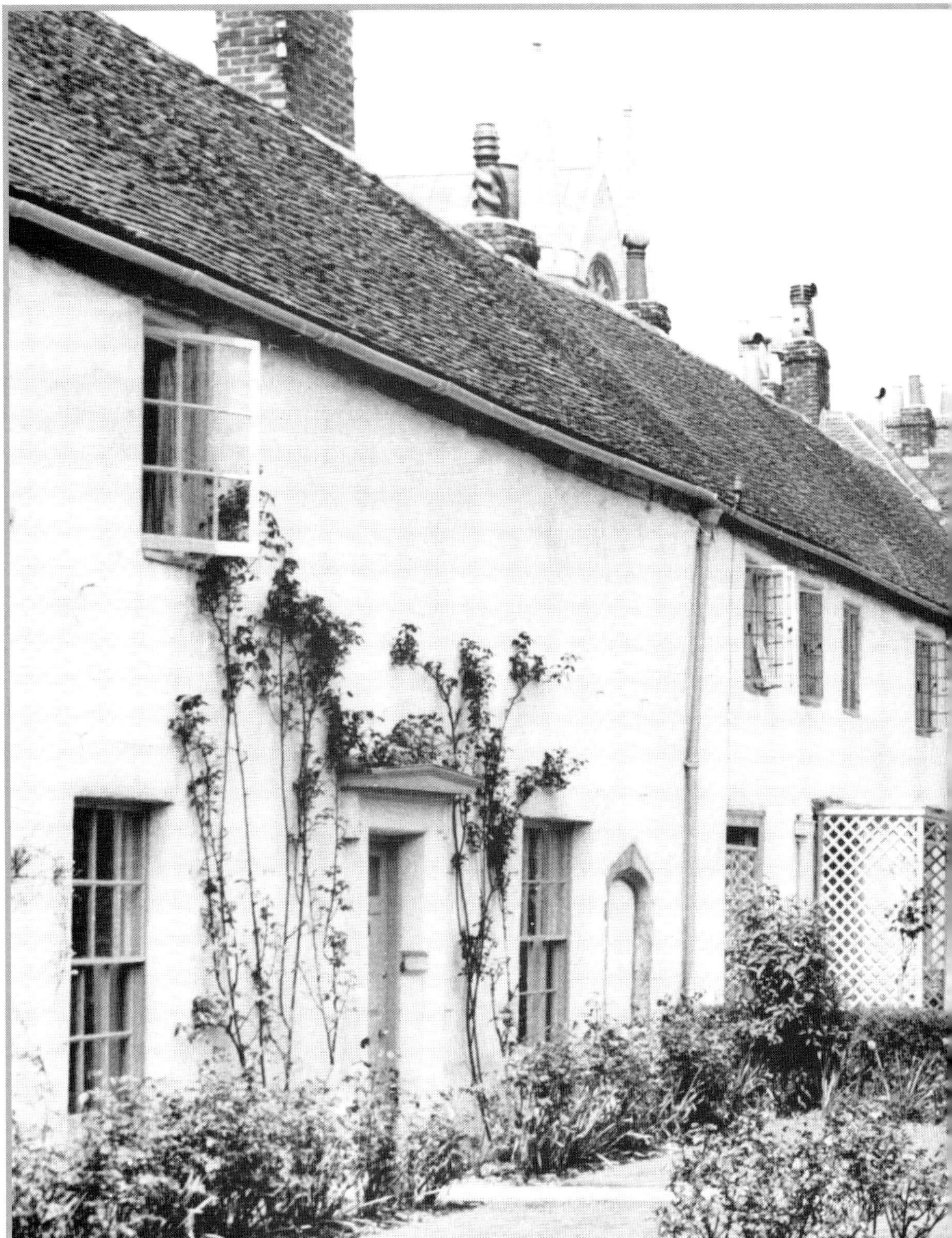

Vicars Close c1960 C84077
Some 15th-century archways are visible, which give a clue to the houses' medieval origins and counter the 1825 stuccoing, windows and doorways. To the right is the 1825 flint wall separating the west range from the eastern range shop conversions. At the end is the splendid 14th-century Vicars' Hall built for the vicars choral.

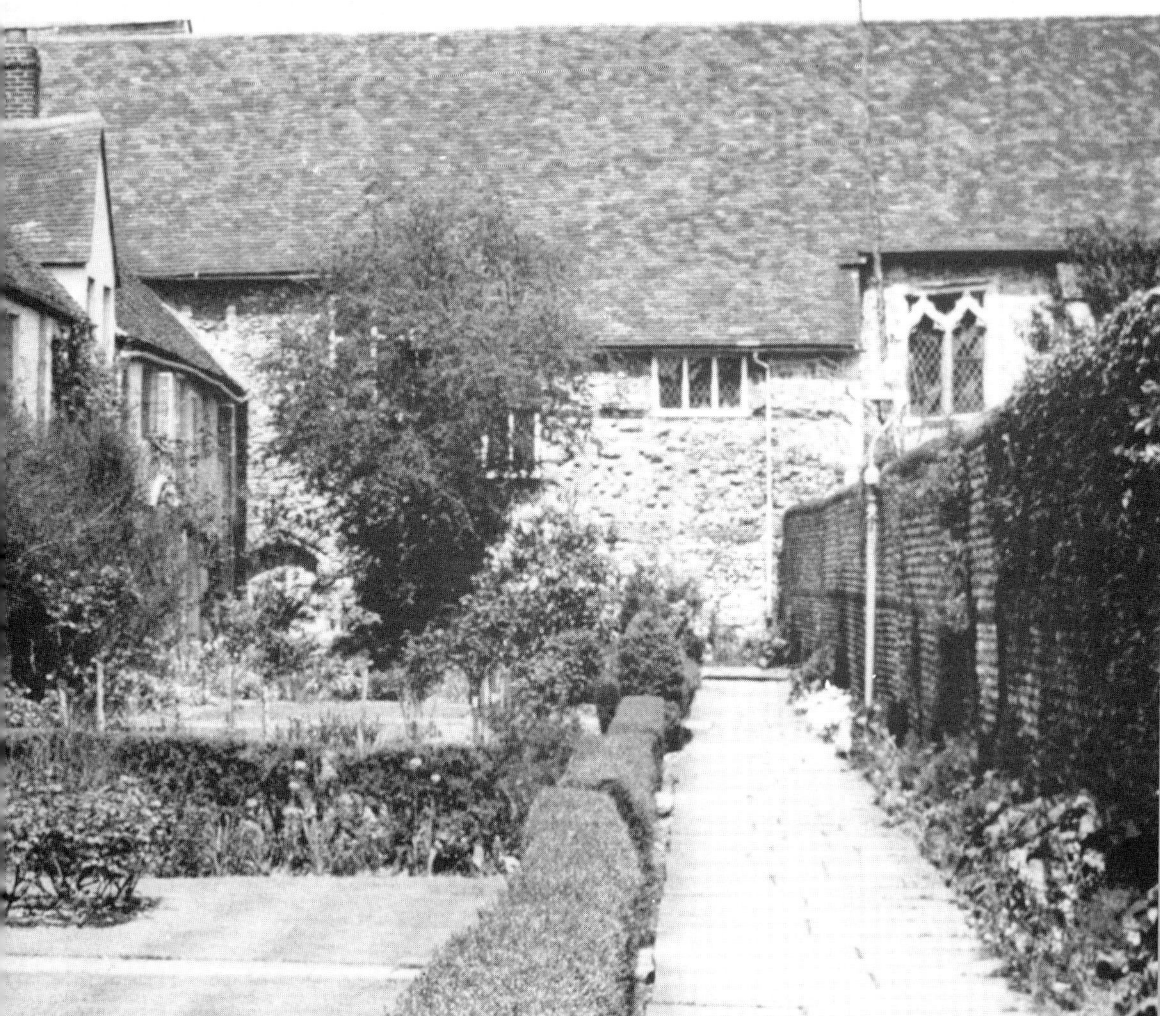

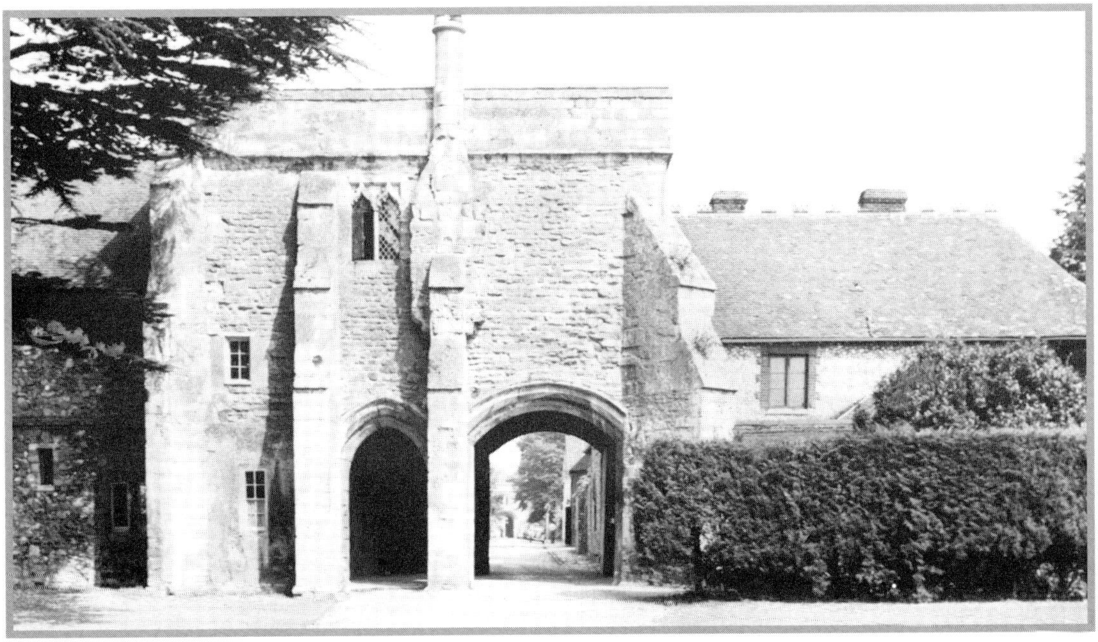

ENTRANCE TO THE BISHOP'S PALACE C1960 C84065
This view, taken from the Bishop's Palace garden, looks through its gateway into Canon Lane. The Palace gatehouse was built about 1327, and its upper storey is said to have been used as a prison for sinning priests and heretics at one stage in its history.

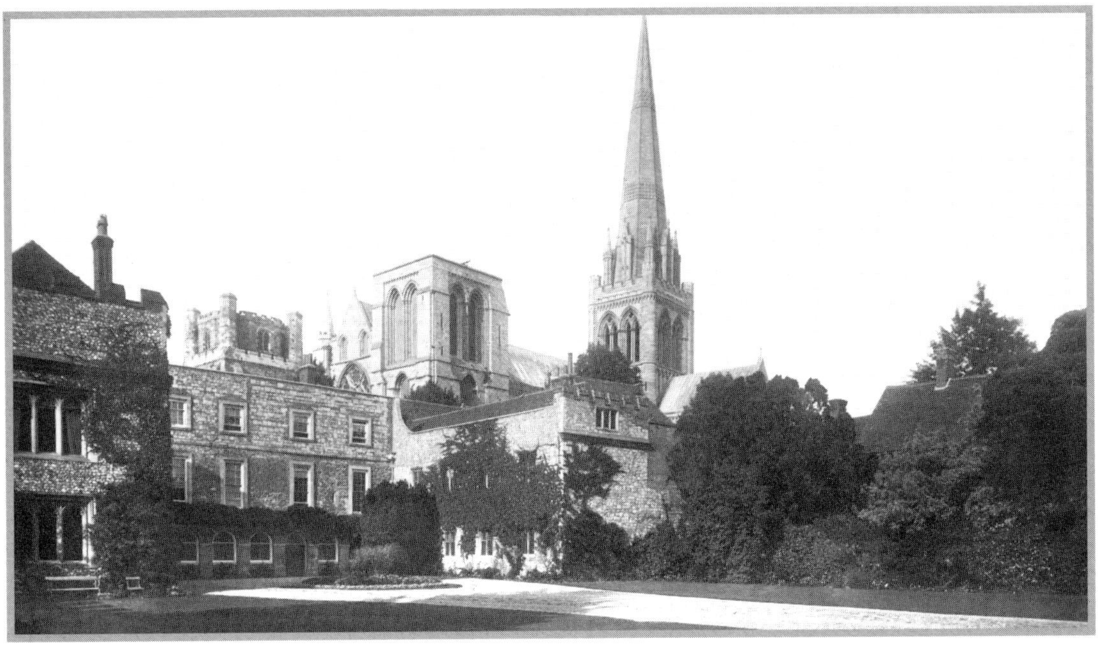

THE CATHEDRAL AND THE BISHOP'S PALACE 1892 29986
The Palace, set in tranquil and beautiful grounds, is not the most grandiose of bishop's residences. It is a rambling medieval house with side wings; its centre was given sash windows and coped parapets in the 1720s. Its chief glory, not seen here, is the early 13th-century chapel.

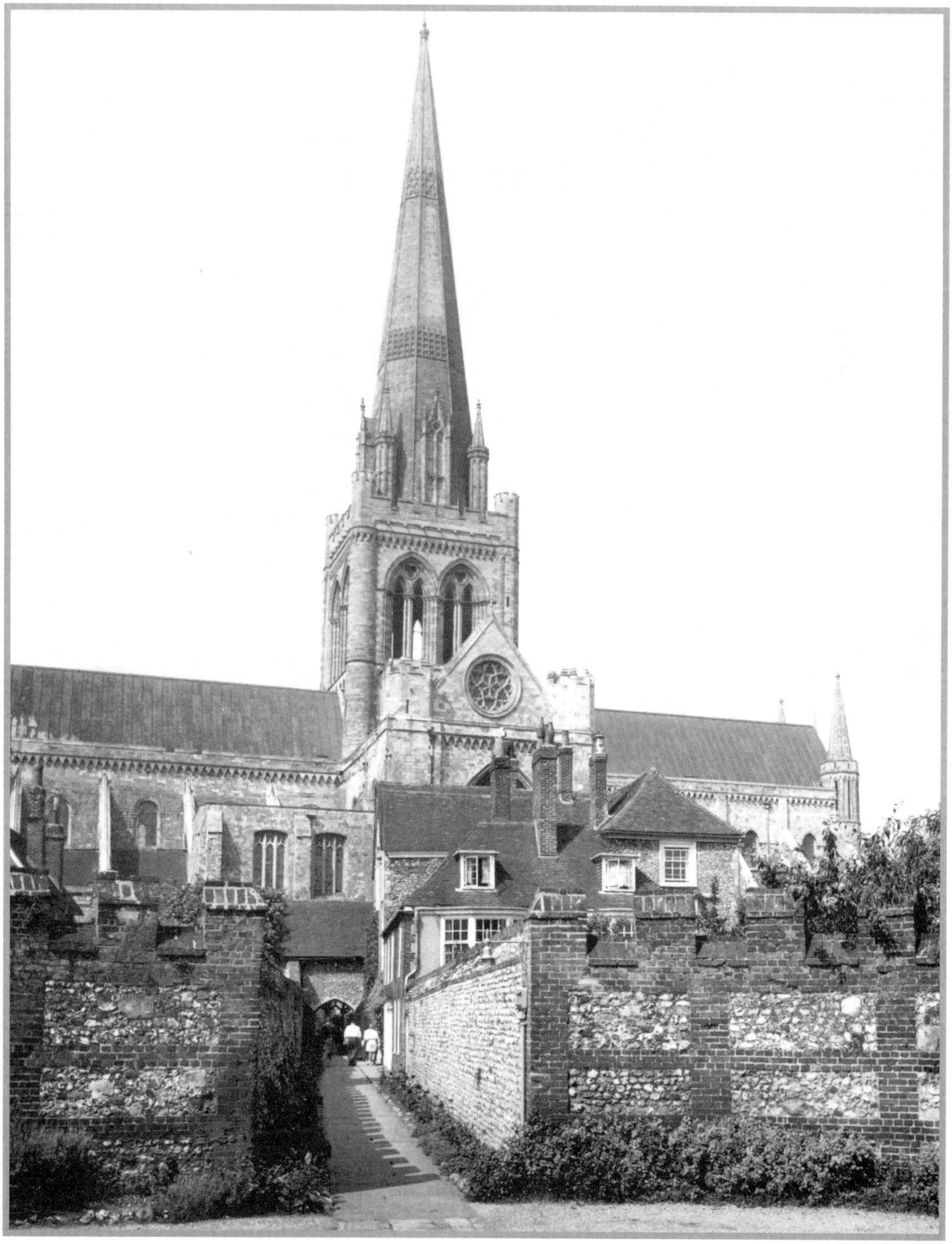

THE CATHEDRAL c1960 C84066

This is one of the most well-known viewpoints of the cathedral, from Canon Lane in front of The Deanery looking along St Richard's Walk, which leads into the cloisters. The spire and central tower were entirely rebuilt after they collapsed into the body of the church in 1861.

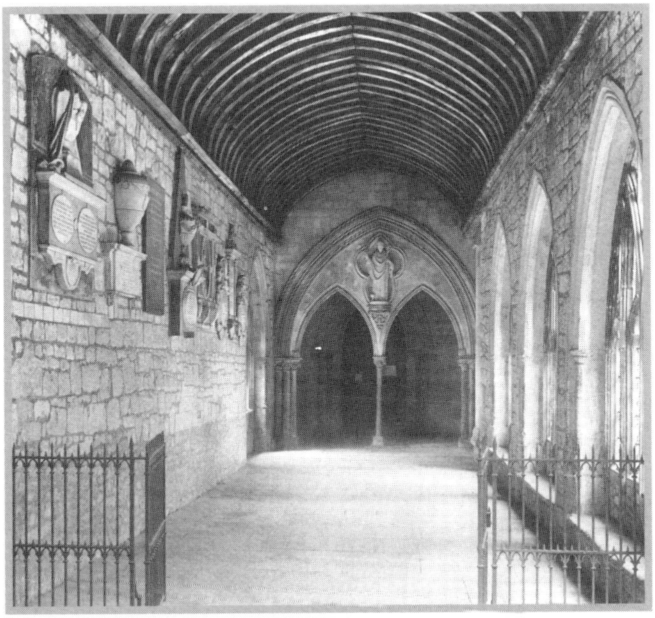

THE CATHEDRAL CLOISTERS AND ST.RICHARD'S PORCH 1892 29995

THE CATHEDRAL CLOISTERS AND ST.RICHARD'S PORCH 1892

Despite having a three-sided cloister, the cathedral was not a monastic foundation, so the cloisters serve to enclose a tranquil grassy area known as The Paradise. St Richard, whose brightly-painted statue is in the niche above the double arch, was bishop from 1245 to 1253 and canonised by the pope in 1262.

THE CATHEDRAL
West Front 1906

This view is not a public one, having been taken in the Prebendal School grounds. It shows the cathedral's twin west towers, the south one partially rebuilt in the early 13th century after a storm in 1210, the other in 1900 after being ruinous since collapsing in 1636. To the left is the detached bell tower.

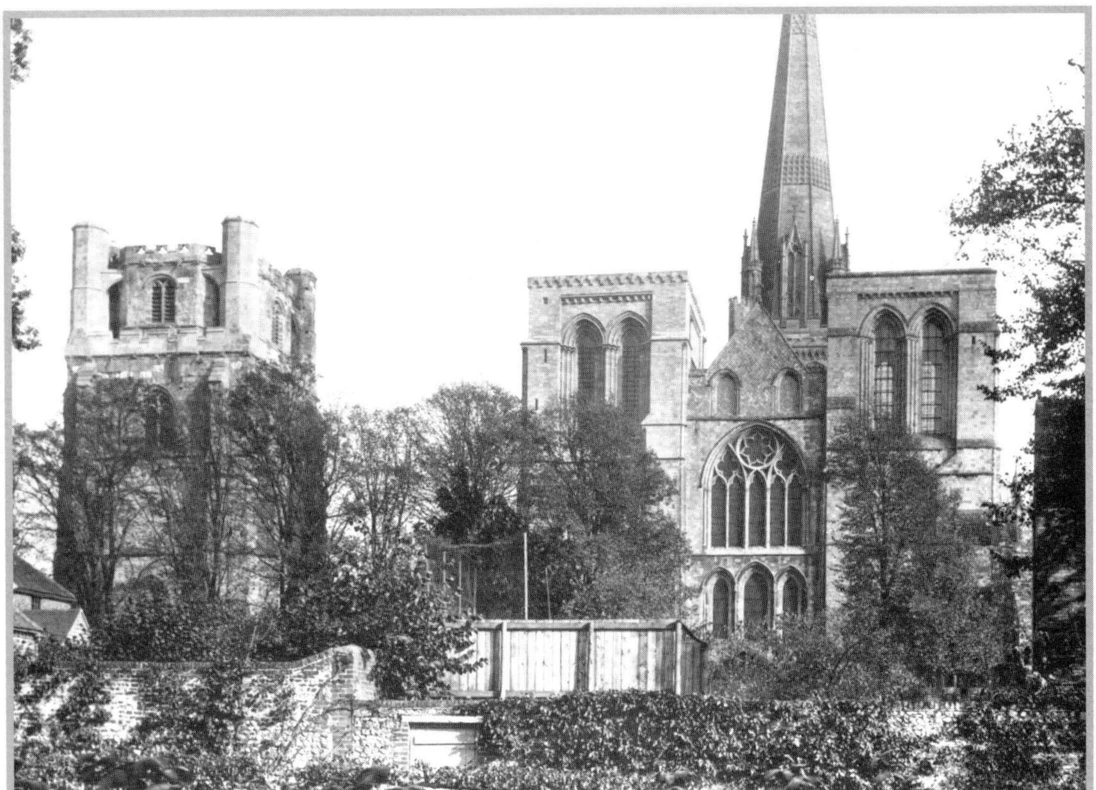

THE CATHEDRAL, WEST FRONT 1906 55029

THE BELL TOWER 1892
The detached bell tower was built to carry the bells because the cathedral's central tower had become too weak to allow the bells to be rung. Suitably massive, the bell tower was started about 1375, but was not completed until about 1440; in 1873 it suffered the indignity of being proposed for conversion to a municipal water tower.

THE CATHEDRAL
from the North East 1892
Apart from the removal of most of the gravestones, this view is little changed. The whole of the cathedral's north front is seen from West Street, although this was not always the case: a row of houses was demolished in the 18th century in order to open up the view.

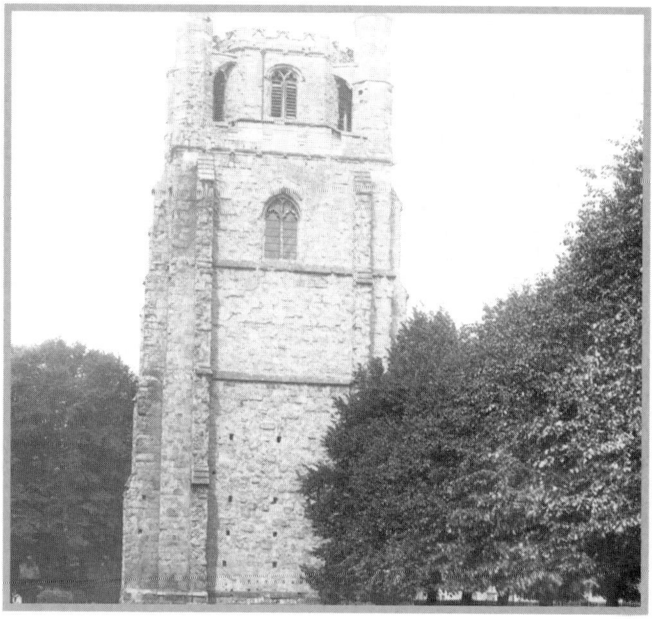

THE BELL TOWER 1892 30001

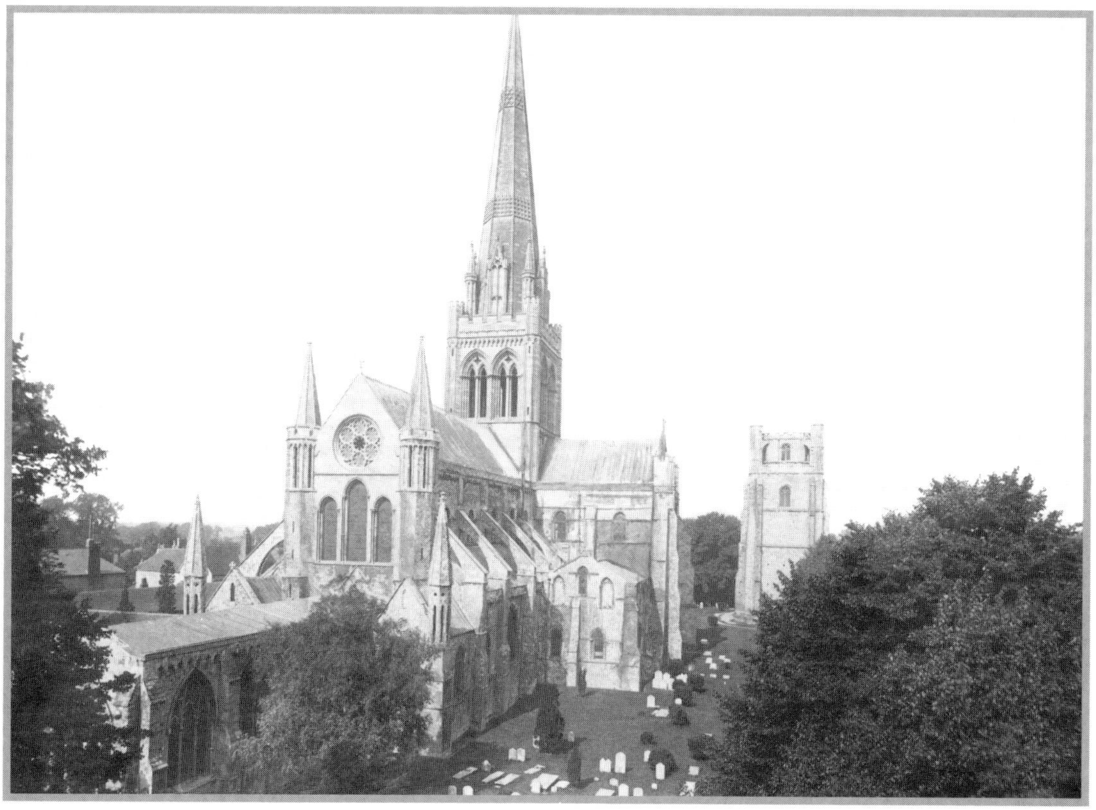

THE CATHEDRAL, FROM THE NORTH EAST 1892 29985

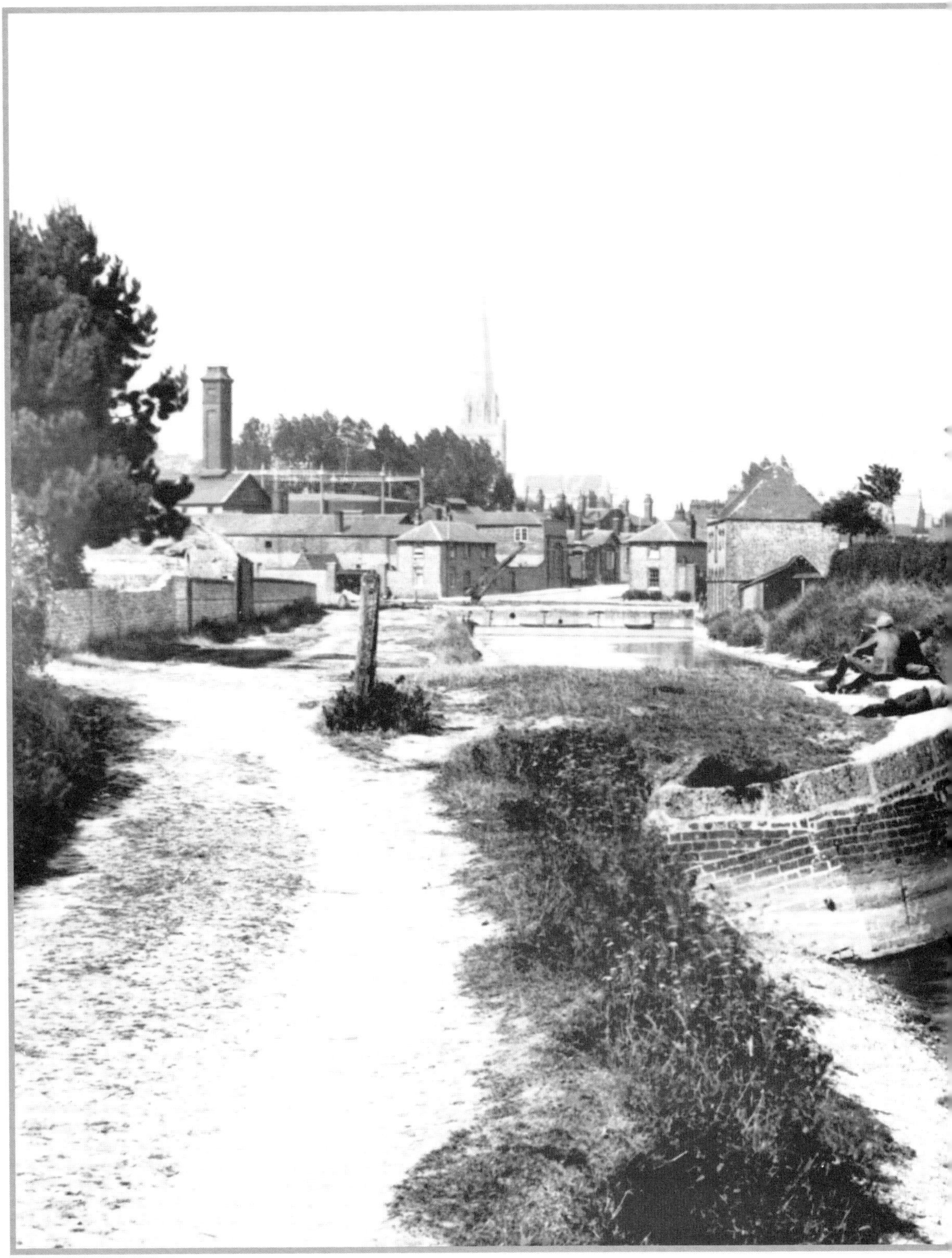

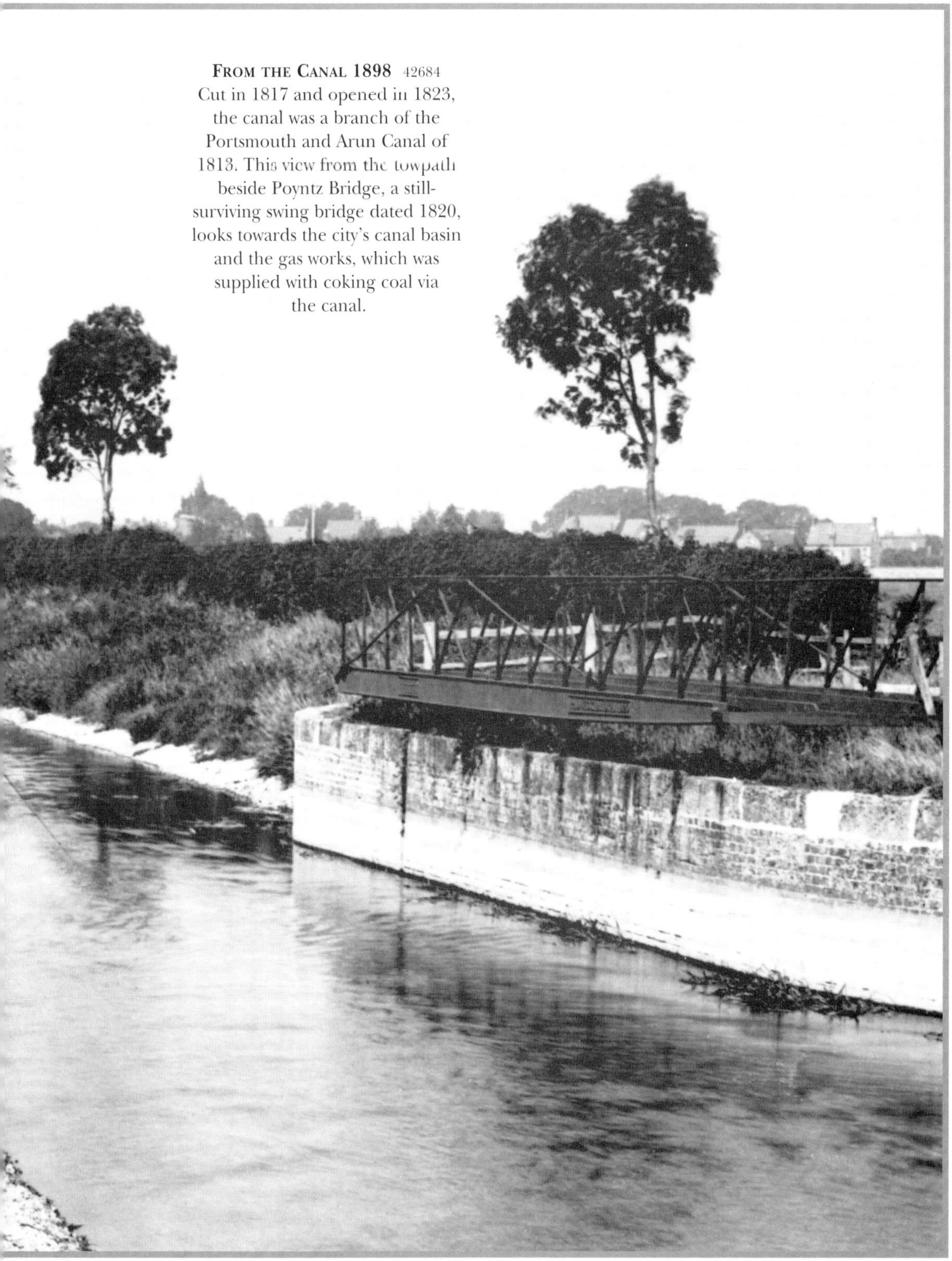

From the Canal 1898 42684
Cut in 1817 and opened in 1823, the canal was a branch of the Portsmouth and Arun Canal of 1813. This view from the towpath beside Poyntz Bridge, a still-surviving swing bridge dated 1820, looks towards the city's canal basin and the gas works, which was supplied with coking coal via the canal.

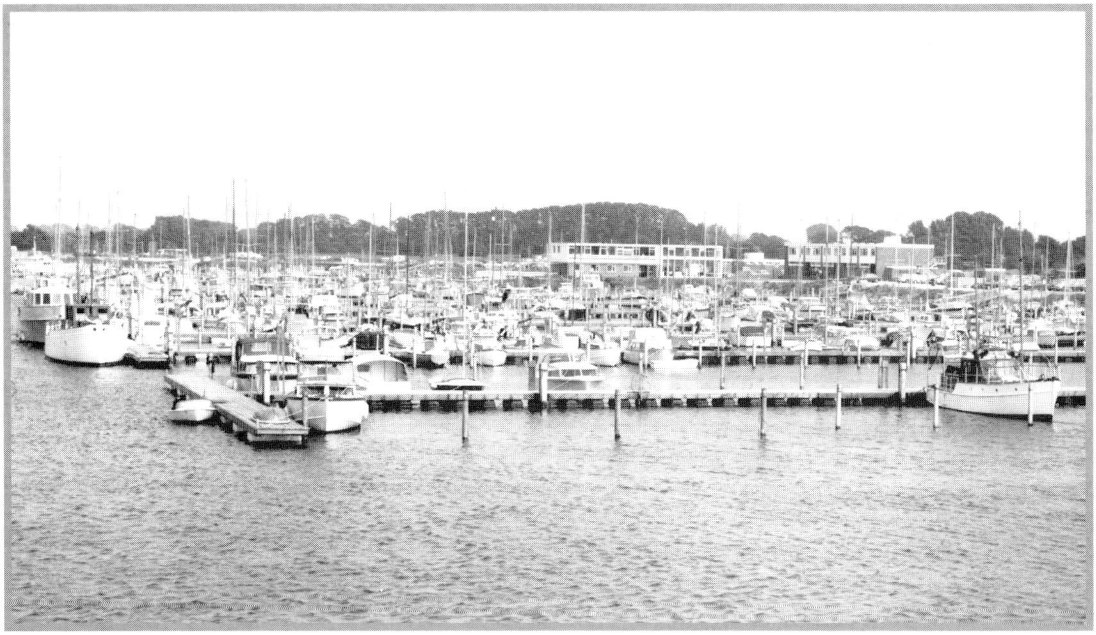

THE YACHT BASIN FROM THE WATCH TOWER c1965 C84177
Where the Portsmouth to Arun Canal, opened in 1813, reached the estuaries east of Portsmouth, a lock was formed and a canal basin built. This is the basis of the Chichester Marina, which grew up immediately north of Salterns Lock to serve the leisure sailing and boating for which this area is now famous.

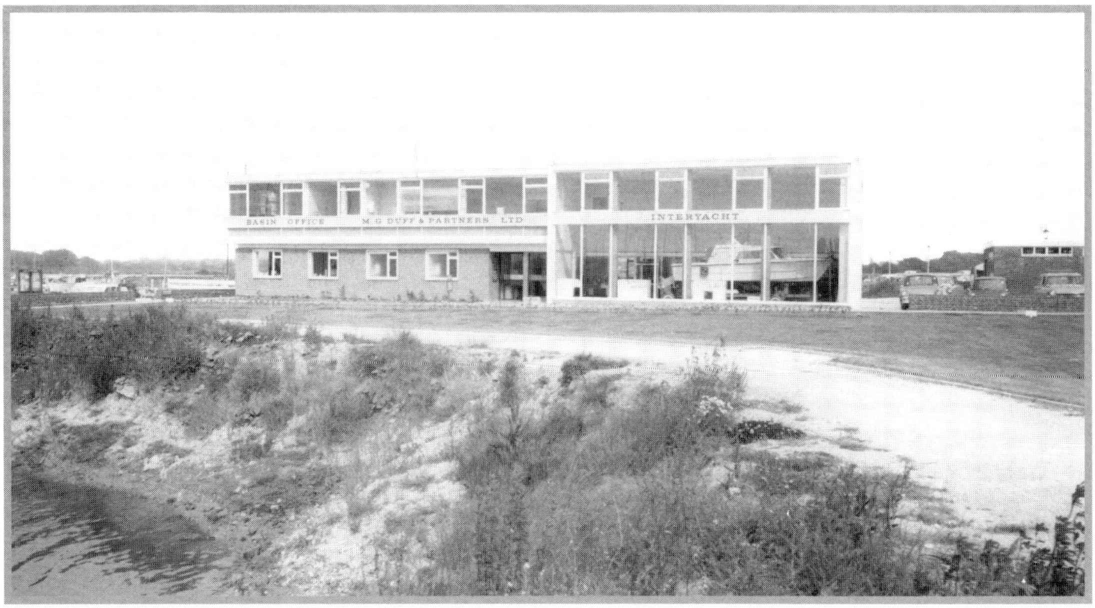

THE YACHT BASIN c1965 C84167
This building, brand new in 1965, has been improved by the addition of a pitched tiled roof, and the area in front has been landscaped and planted most attractively. To the right, another 1960s building has been improved by the addition of conservatories to form shops and a pub, The Spinnaker, which serve the marina berth holders and visitors.

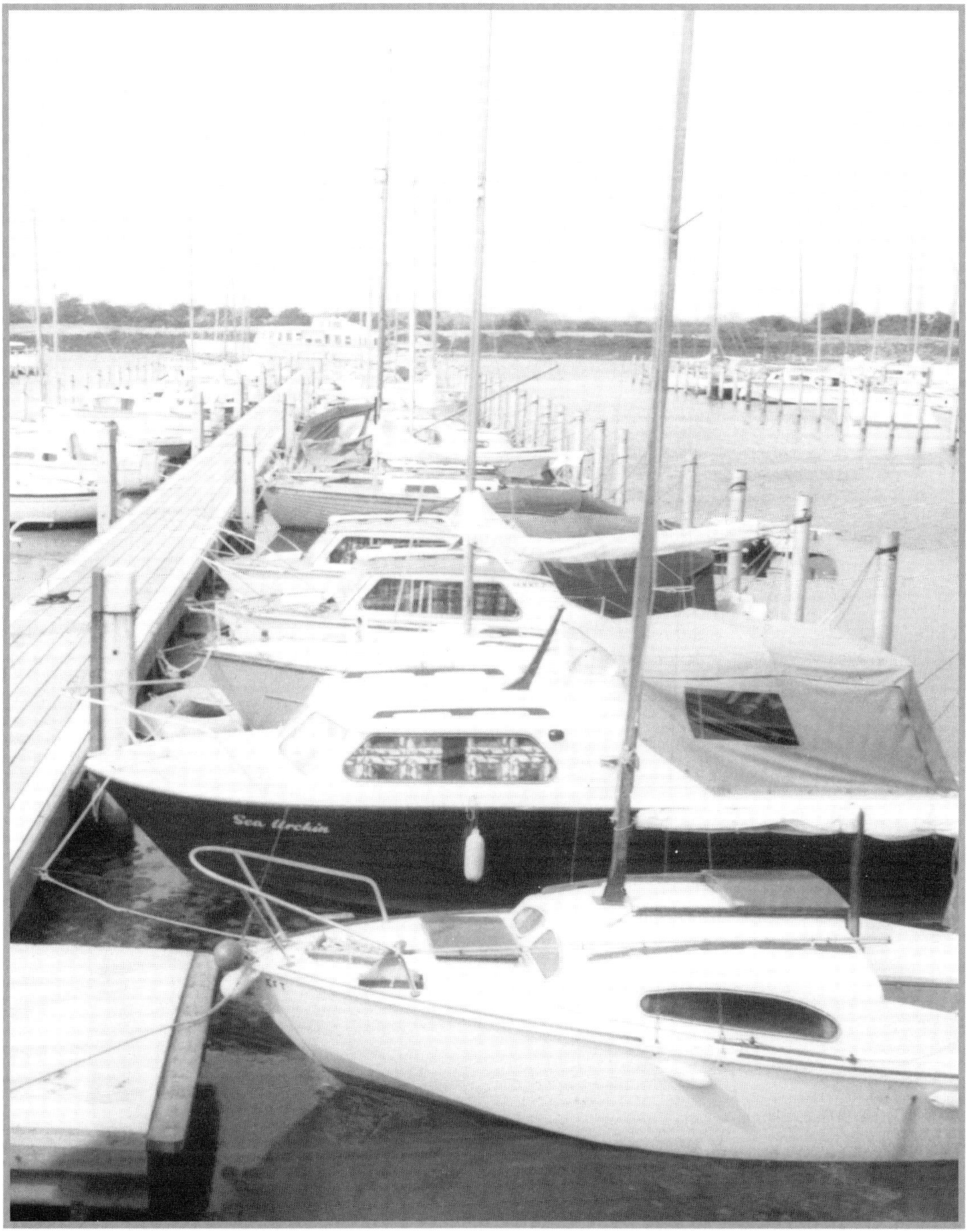

The Yacht Basin c1965 C84173
Seeing all these leisure boats berthed (nowadays larger and more luxurious ones) one wonders how many people realise that the basin started life as the terminus for a canal, whose promoters in their 1817 prospectus gave one of their principal aims as 'the improvement and better cultivation of the circumjacent country by the conveyance of manure'.

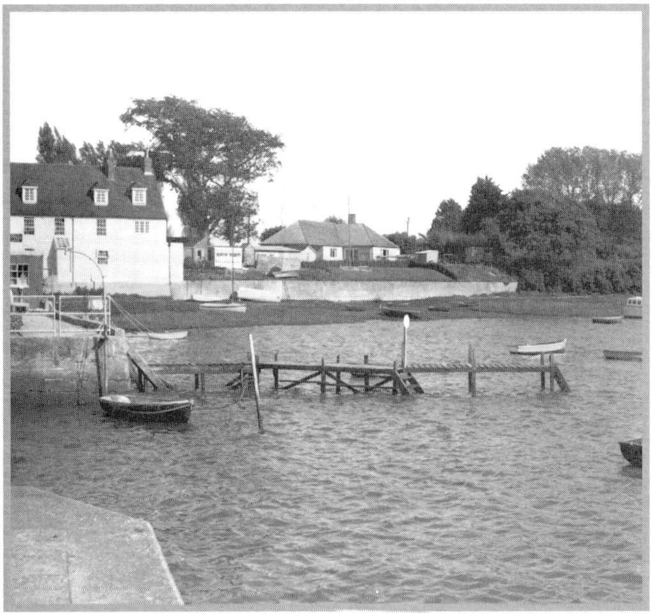

DELL QUAY c1960 D244040

DELL QUAY c1960

Dell Quay was another of the little ports that are or were dotted along the shore of the estuaries west of Chichester: Chichester Harbour, Langstone Harbour and Portsmouth Harbour. Chichester Harbour mostly handled agricultural produce, coal and coastal trade and provided shelter from storms in the English Channel. Portsmouth Harbour, of course, fried bigger fish altogether.

DELL QUAY c1965

The quay itself is mostly occupied by Dell Quay Sailing Club: there is no trade, but its small warehouse survives. This view looks east from the quay towards the thriving Crown and Anchor pub which itself looks out over the estuary, here at its prettiest with woods and expansive views.

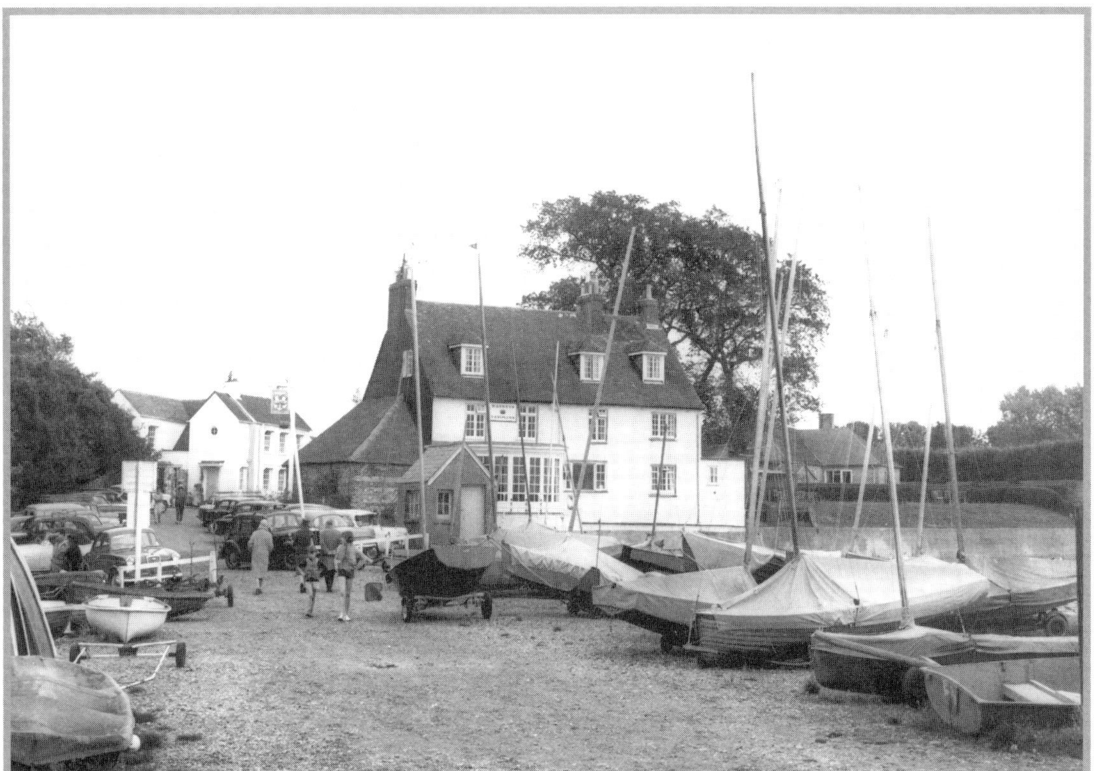

DELL QUAY c1965 D244144

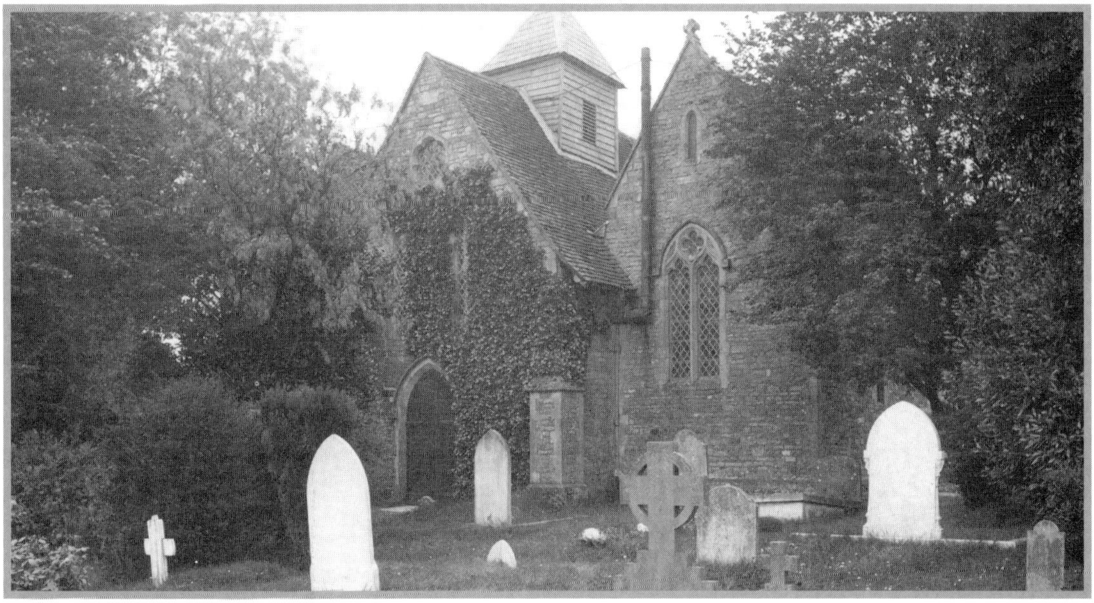

Fishbourne, The Church 1906 55725
Before the Roman palace was discovered Fishbourne was noted for its tide mill, now long gone, and its watermill, converted to flats in 1958, which were at the head of the Fishbourne Channel of Chichester Harbour. The main Portsmouth Road, the A27, caused the village to migrate north-west from the medieval parish church, which sits in isolation near the manor house.

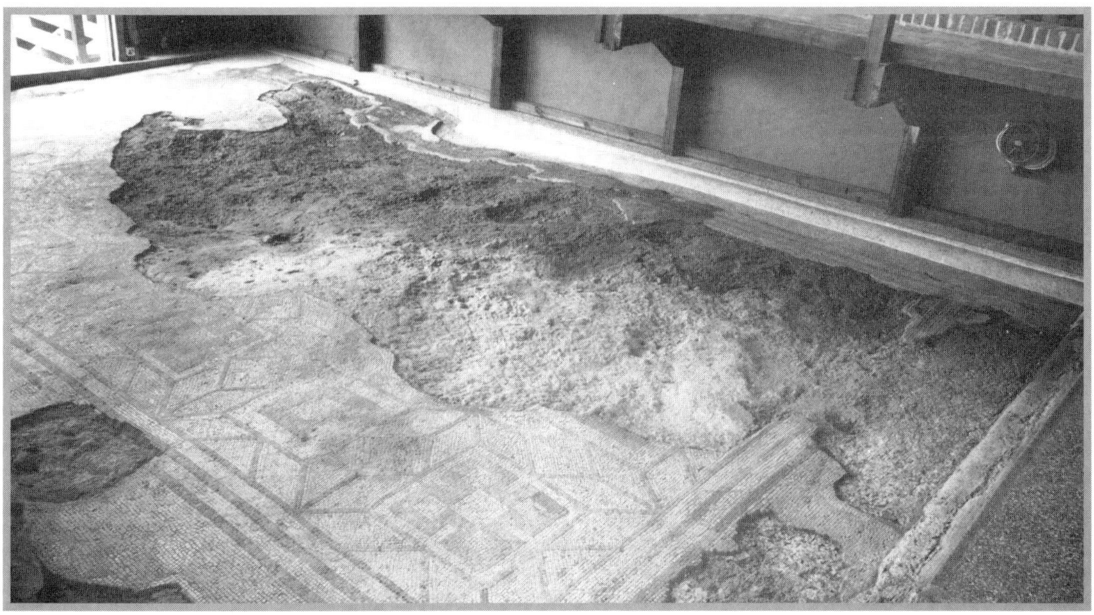

Fishbourne, The Roman Palace c1960 F132021
In 1960 Fishbourne was well and truly put on the map when excavation for a water main uncovered mosaics. What was revealed was an extraordinarily important archaeological discovery: the palace, dating from about 75 AD, of the pro-Roman Tiberius Claudius Cogidubnus, King of the Celtic Regnenses, styled King and Legate to the Roman Emperor in Britannia.

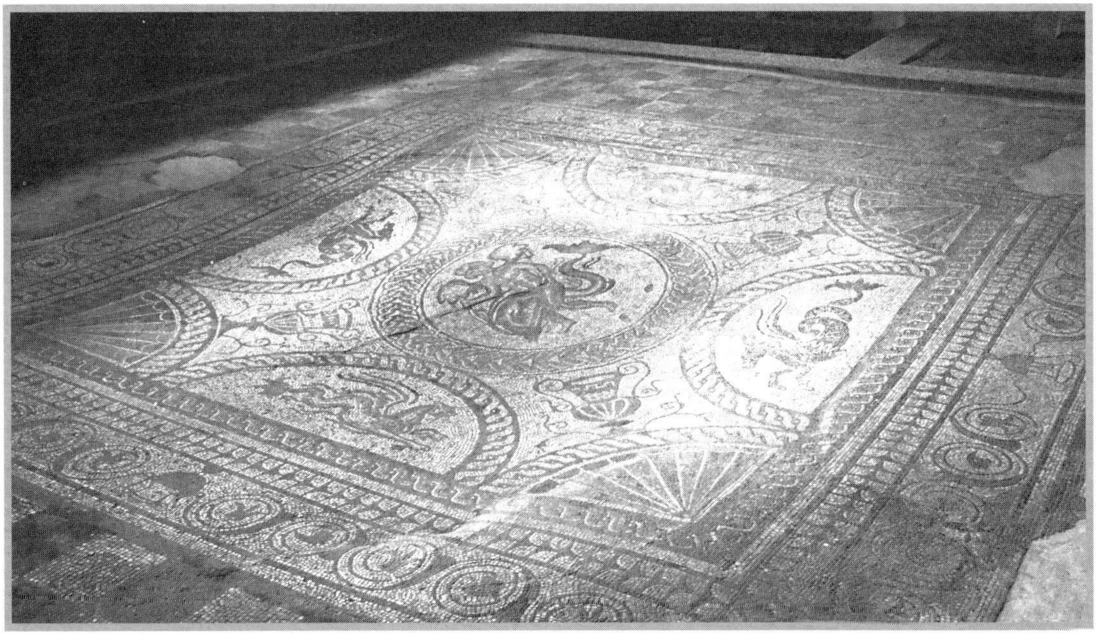

FISHBOURNE, THE ROMAN PALACE c1960 F132002
The palace was as large as any in Rome itself, and had work of the highest quality. This view shows one of the best of the mosaic floors with its centre piece of Cupid riding a dolphin. Enough evidence was also found to allow parts of the original gardens to be reconstructed.

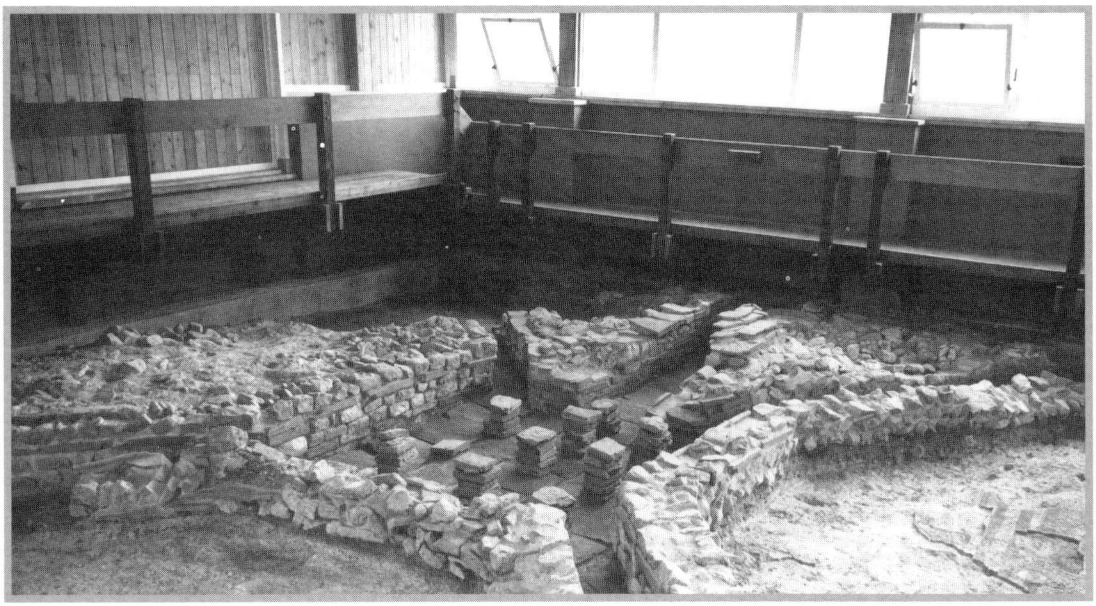

FISHBOURNE, THE ROMAN PALACE c1960 F132017
The palace had underfloor hot air heating; this view, within the buildings erected to protect the excavations, shows the hypocaust ducts, as the floor itself has gone. The plan of the palace was of a huge central garden surrounded by stone buildings with another open court surrounding luxurious gardens which ran down to the sea.

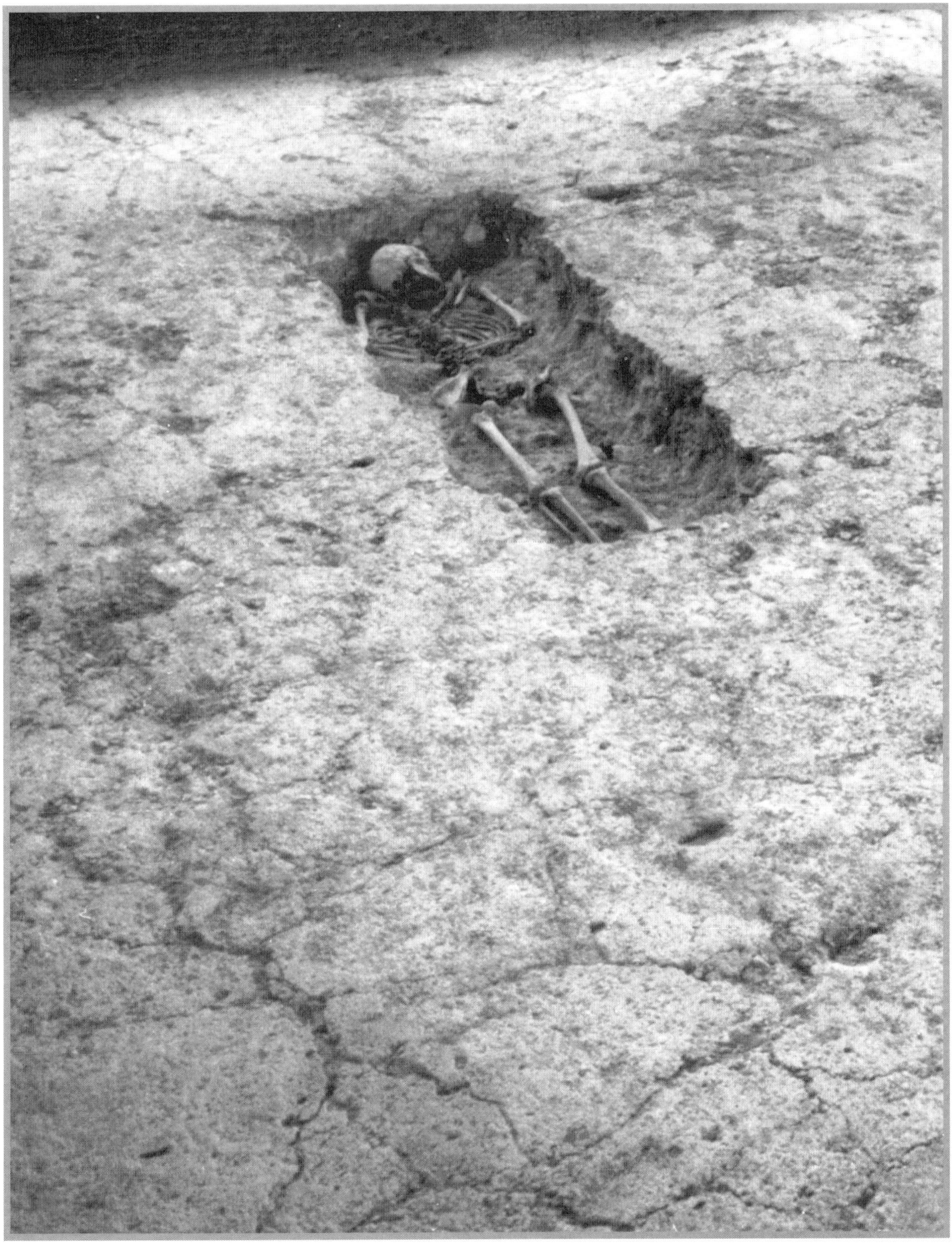

FISHBOURNE, THE ROMAN PALACE c1960 F132008
More recent finds nearby have included the military supply base for the Roman invading army of 43AD, which under Aulus Plautus Nepos began the conquest of what became Britannia. This presumably indicates the extent of King Cogidubnus' co-operation and the esteem in which he was held by the conquerors.

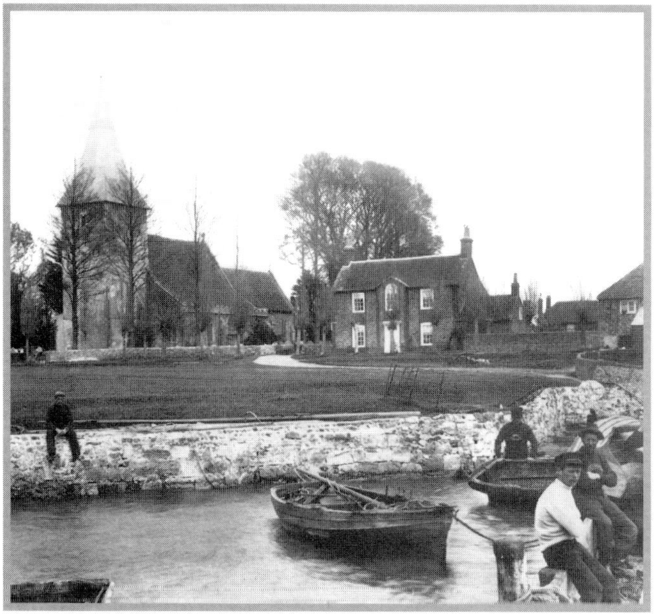

BOSHAM, THE CHURCH AND THE GREEN 1903 50919

BOSHAM
The Church and the Green 1903
Bosham's Anglo-Saxon church has the rare distinction of featuring on the Bayeux Tapestry, that great embroidered record of William the Conqueror's 1066 invasion of England. Bosham was a royal manor, and Earl Harold, later the last Anglo-Danish king of England, is shown praying by a stylised representation of the church before setting off for Normandy in 1064.

BOSHAM
The Church 1901
This view from the field north of the church shows the former farm buildings, now houses. Almost inevitably, this field is now a yacht park. The church tower and nave are early 11th-century with a 15th-century spire added, but there is evidence of an even earlier Roman basilica to be seen inside the church.

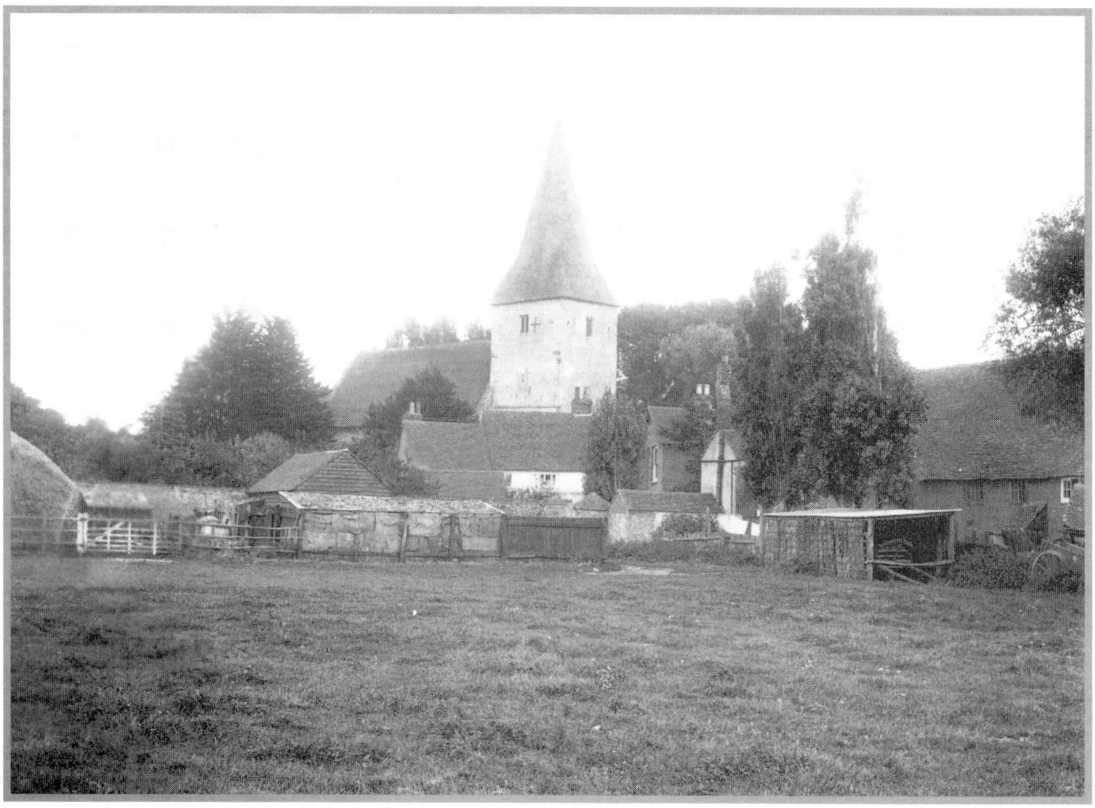

BOSHAM, THE CHURCH 1901 48078

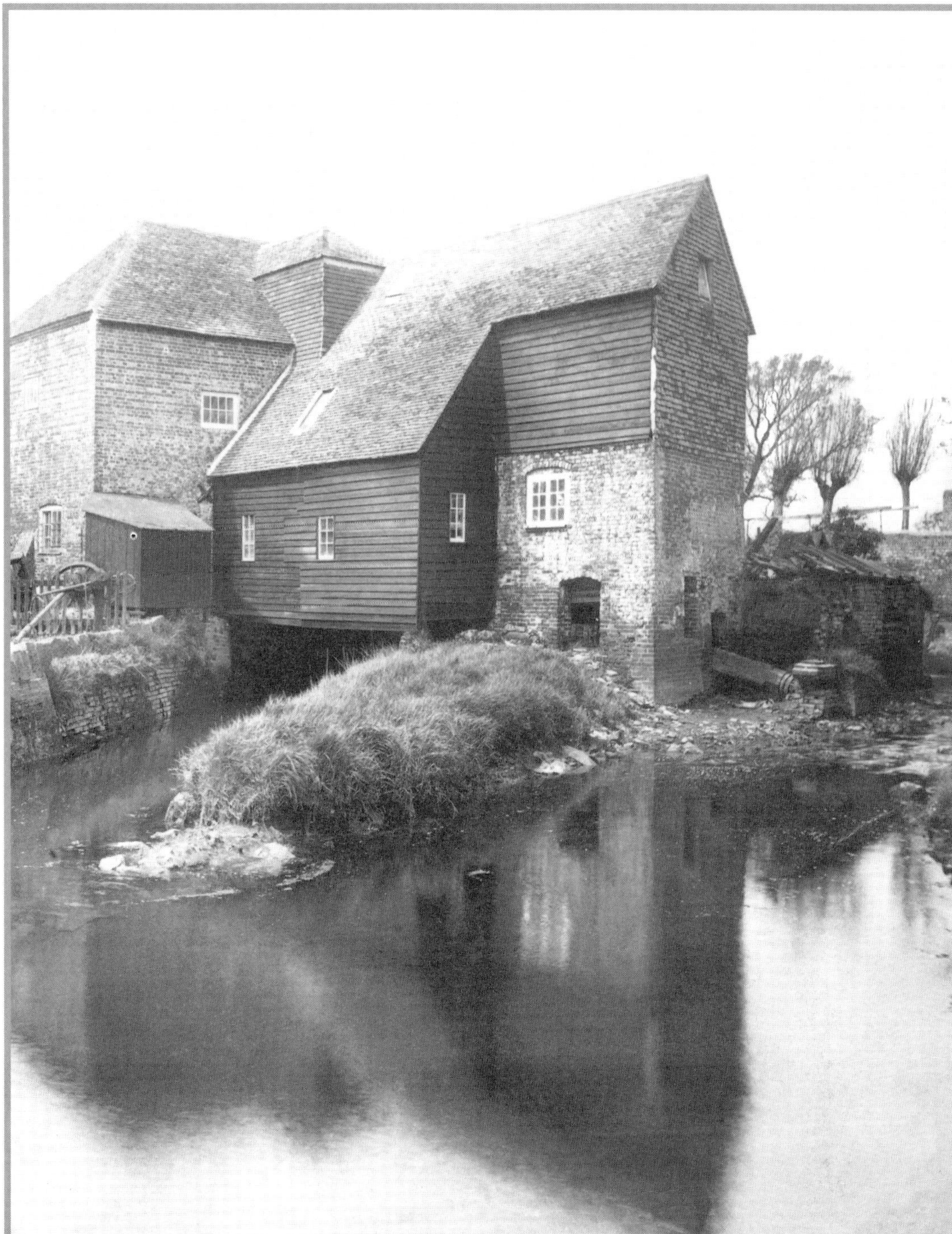

Bosham, The Old Mill 1903 50921
In 1903, of course, the water mill still functioned. Situated south of the church and the green, called Quay Meadow, it was powered via a leet from a mill pond to the north of the church. Now it is the headquarters of the Bosham Yacht Club, and the quays bustle with yachtsmen and boating types.

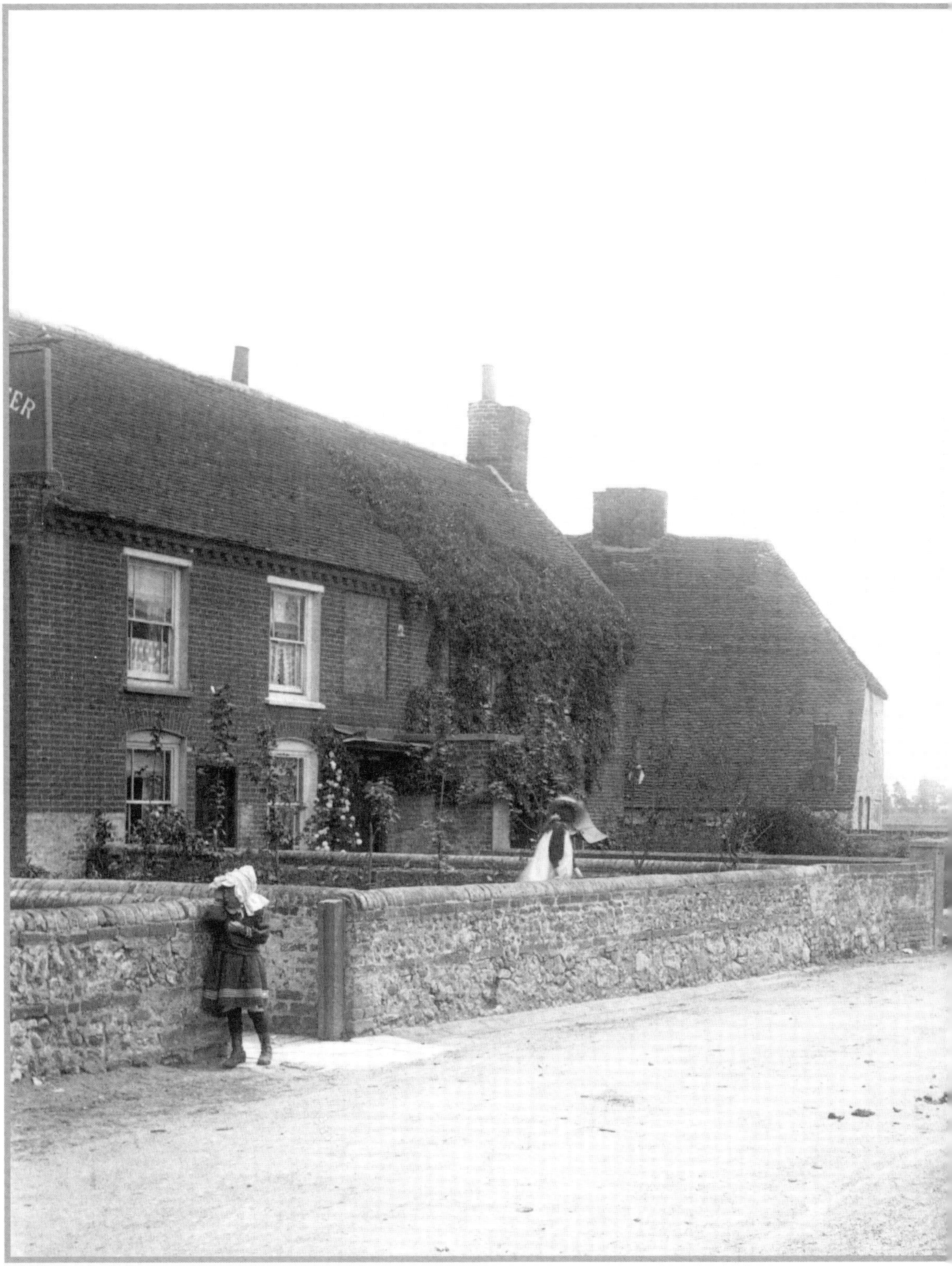
ER

Bosham, The Village 1902 48336
This view looks south to the estuary. The houses on the left survive, including the far one which is dated 1694, but those on the right on either side of the entry to the High Street were rebuilt in the 1950s. Obviously everything is now much more spick and span with pavements, tarmac and undeniably necessary double yellow lines.

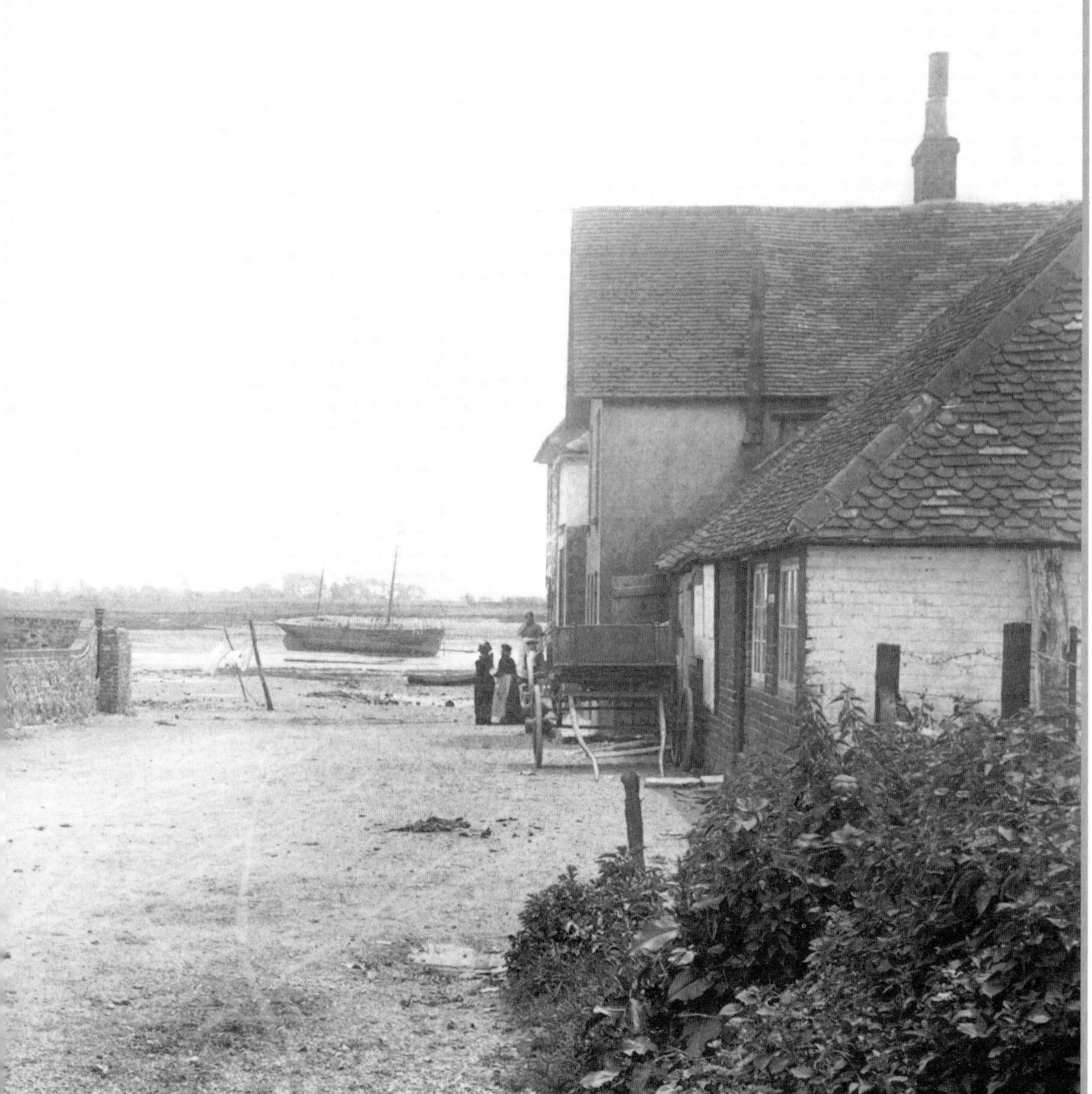

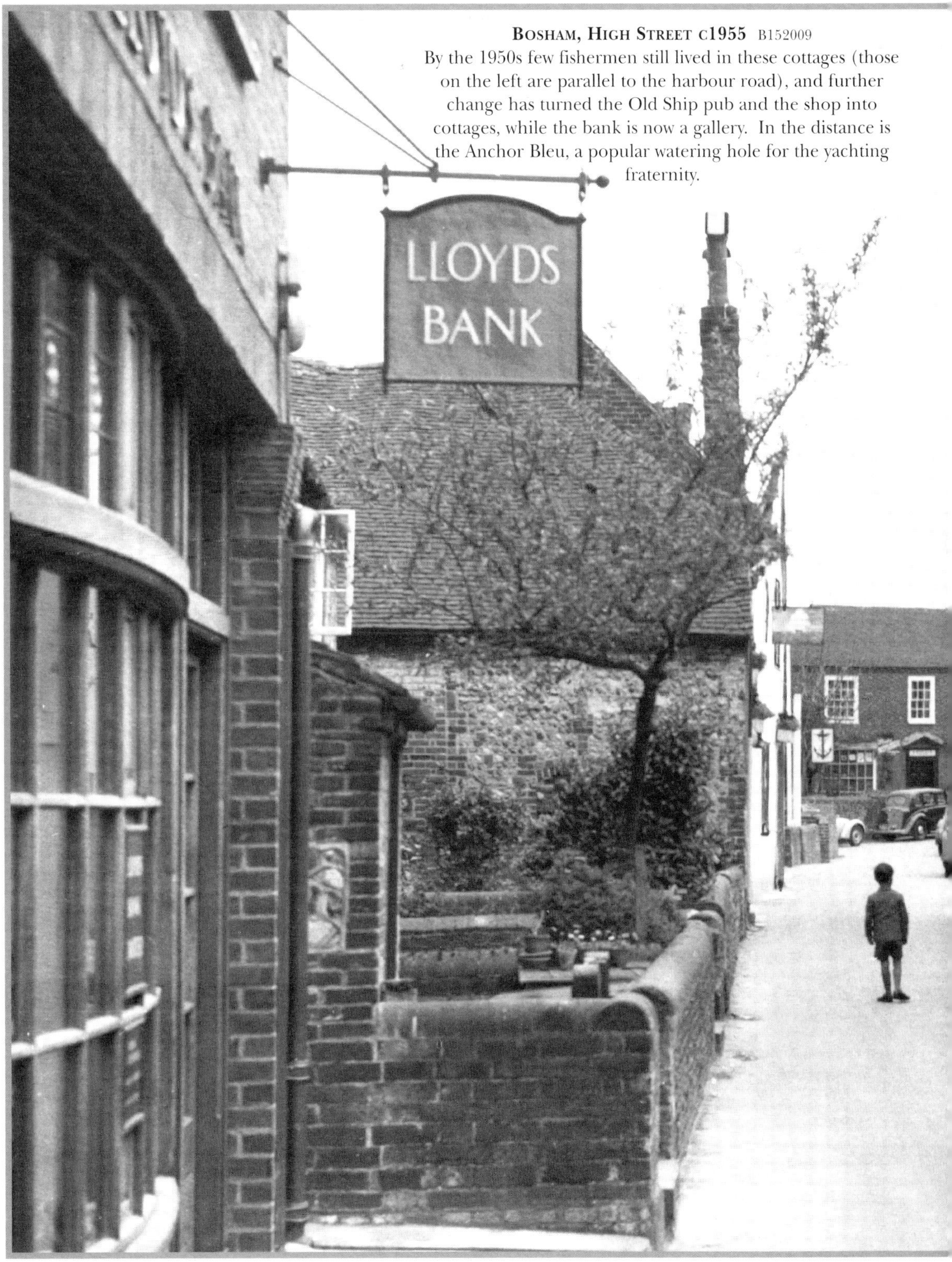

BOSHAM, HIGH STREET C1955 B152009
By the 1950s few fishermen still lived in these cottages (those on the left are parallel to the harbour road), and further change has turned the Old Ship pub and the shop into cottages, while the bank is now a gallery. In the distance is the Anchor Bleu, a popular watering hole for the yachting fraternity.

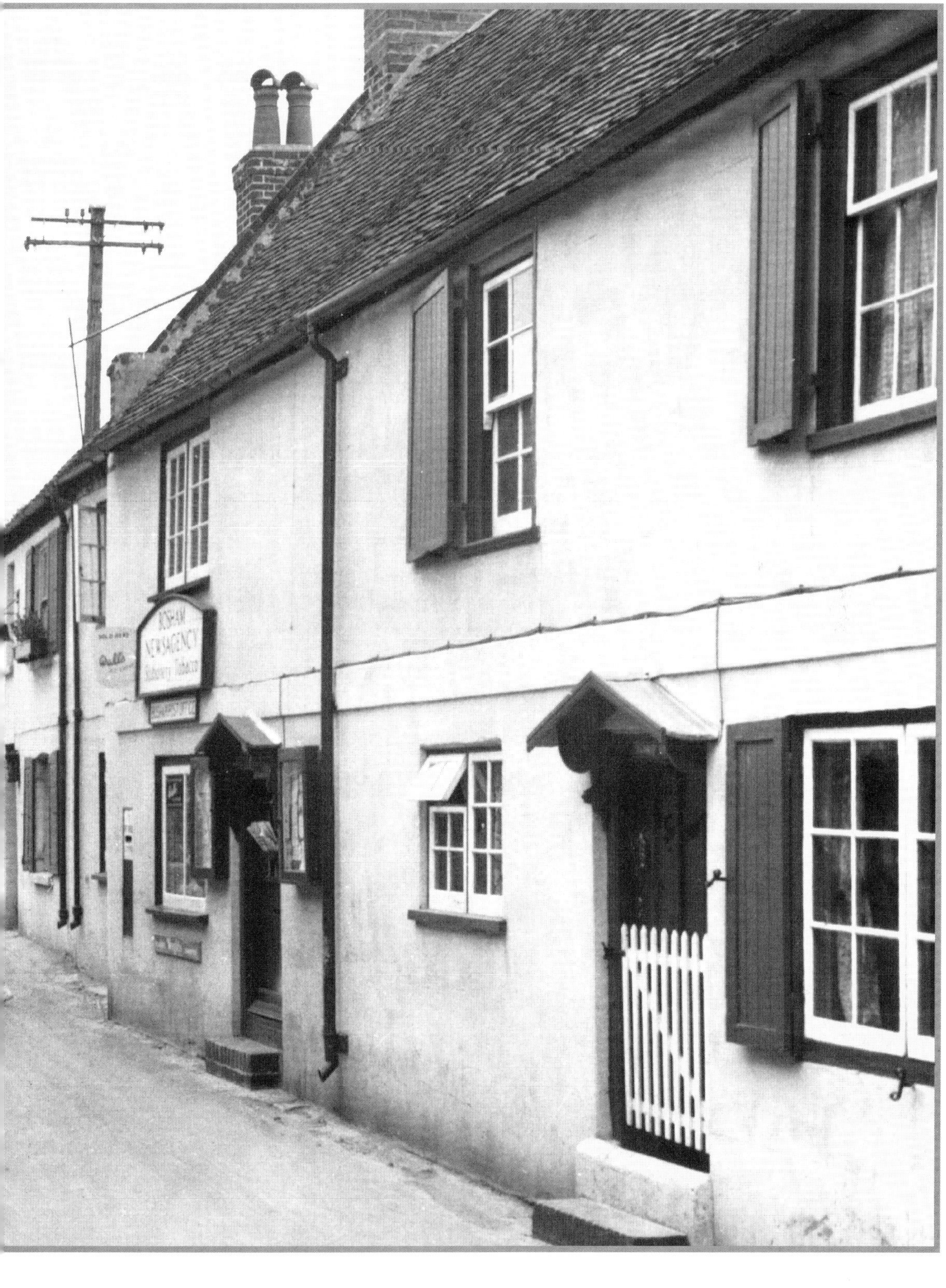
BOSHAM
NEWSAGENCY
Stationery Tobacco

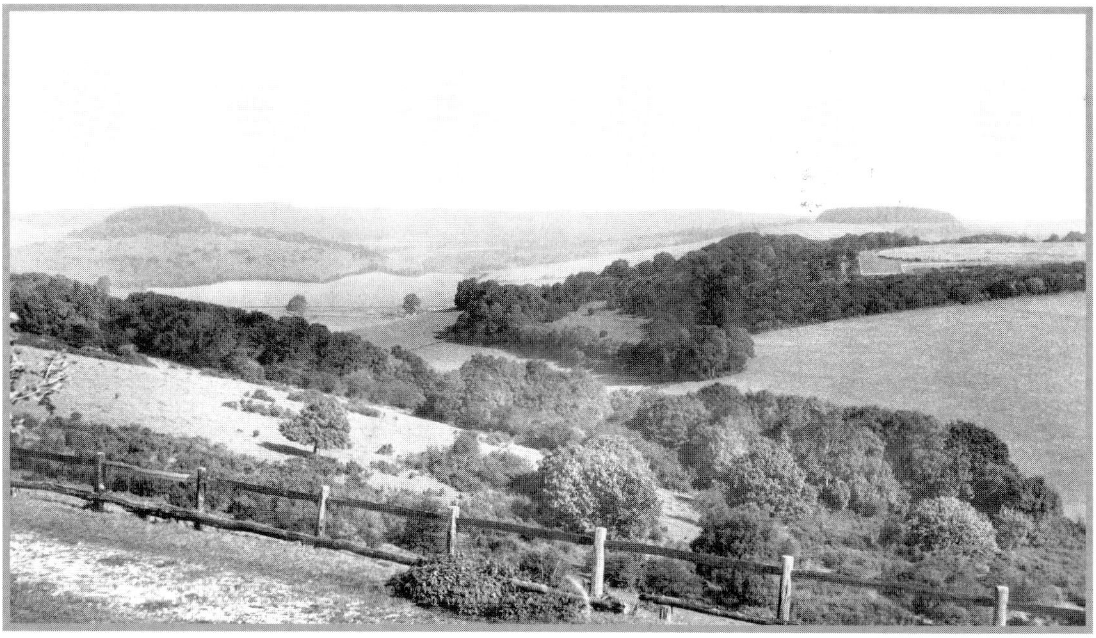

GOODWOOD c1965 C84159
This view, from near The Trundle car park, looks north-west across Charlton Down towards the west end loop of Goodwood race course, and demonstrates very well the open character of the chalk North Downs as they march from east to west a couple of miles north of Chichester on the flat Sussex coastal plain.

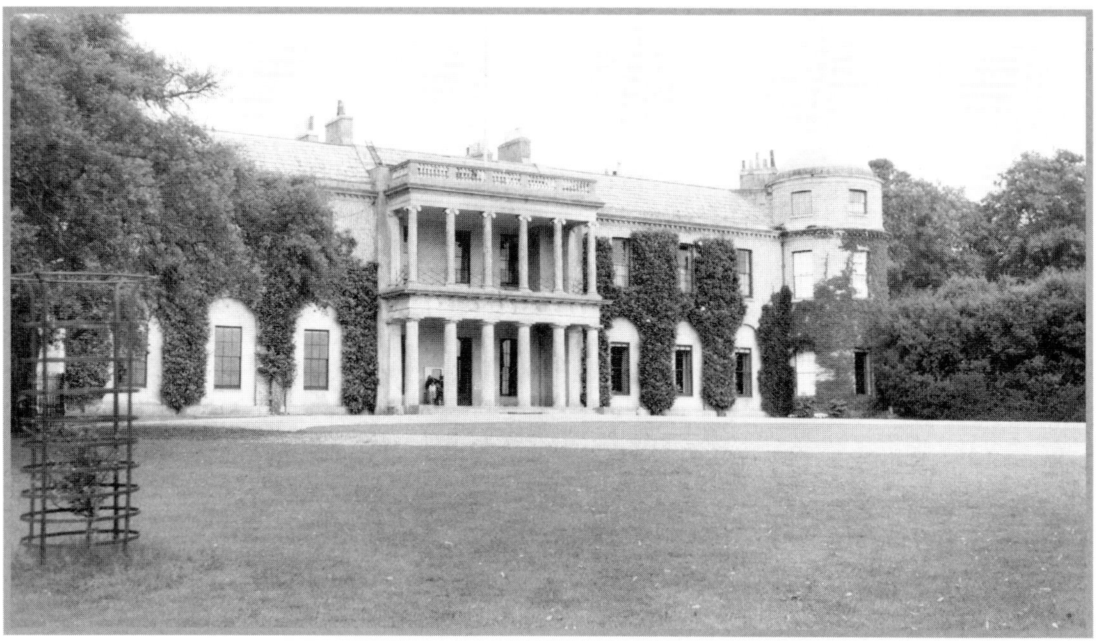

GOODWOOD HOUSE c1965 C84103
Goodwood House itself is on the lowest southern slopes of the chalk Downs at fifty metres above sea level, a hundred metres lower than the racecourse up on its windswept Downs. Set in beautiful landscaped parkland, James Wyatt's south-west front of about 1790 has drum towers and a central two storey portico.

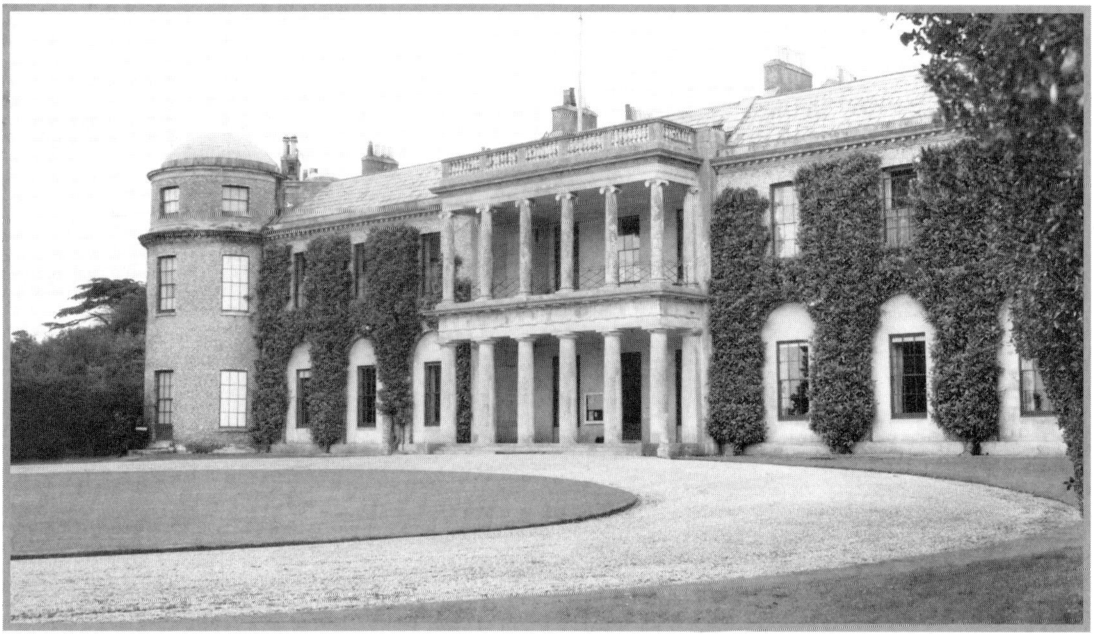

Goodwood House c1965 C84107

Goodwood is the home of the Dukes of Richmond and Gordon. This view shows only one of James Wyatt's three elevations of what would have been an extraordinary octagonal plan around a large central court. The other five ranges were never built. Goodwood is built in flint, unusual in a grand country house.

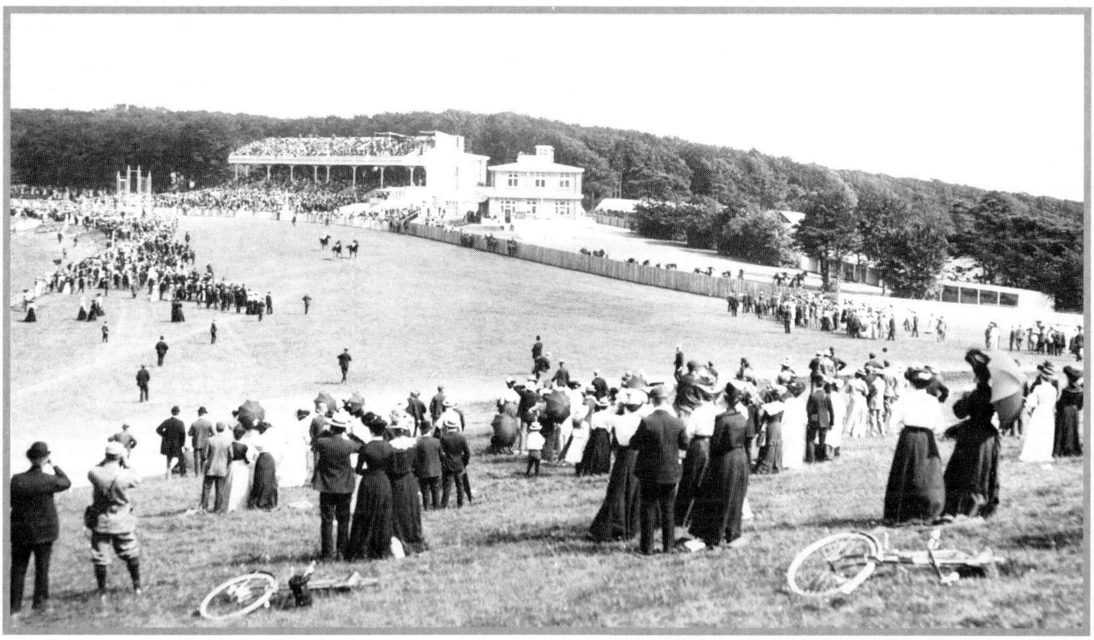

Goodwood House, The Racecourse 1904 52291

Racing was started here on the Downs in 1802 by the Duke of Richmond and Gordon, and the course laid out then has remained virtually unchanged ever since. This view captures the atmosphere of an Edwardian race day with bicycles, boaters, bowlers and plus-fours well to the fore.

GOODWOOD HOUSE, THE RACECOURSE 1904 52290
The race course is wonderfully situated, with vast views across the well-wooded North Downs and south to the sea with Chichester and its cathedral spire in between. It must be one of the most beautifully situated race courses in the country, and 'Glorious Goodwood' is a nickname well earned.

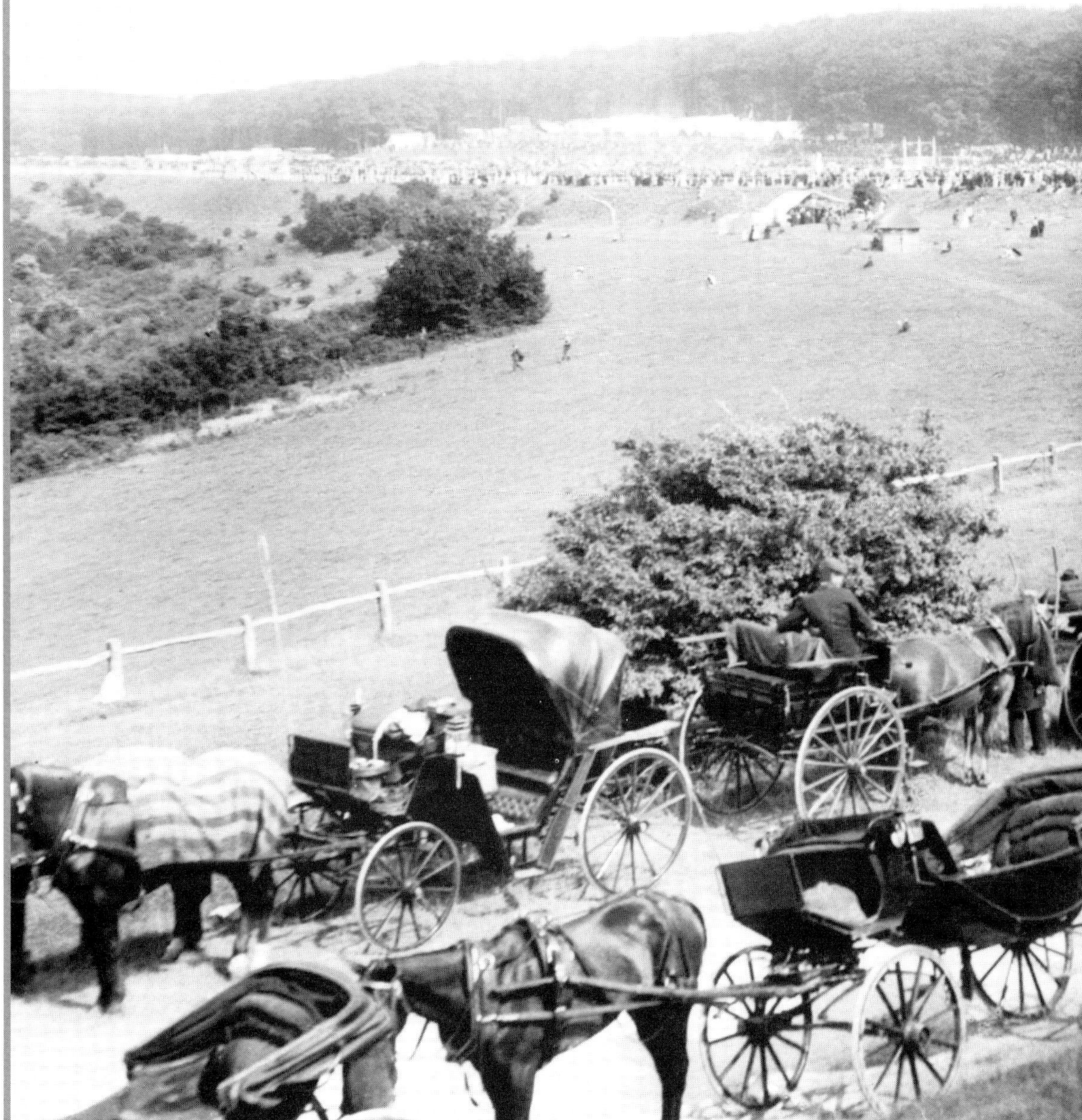

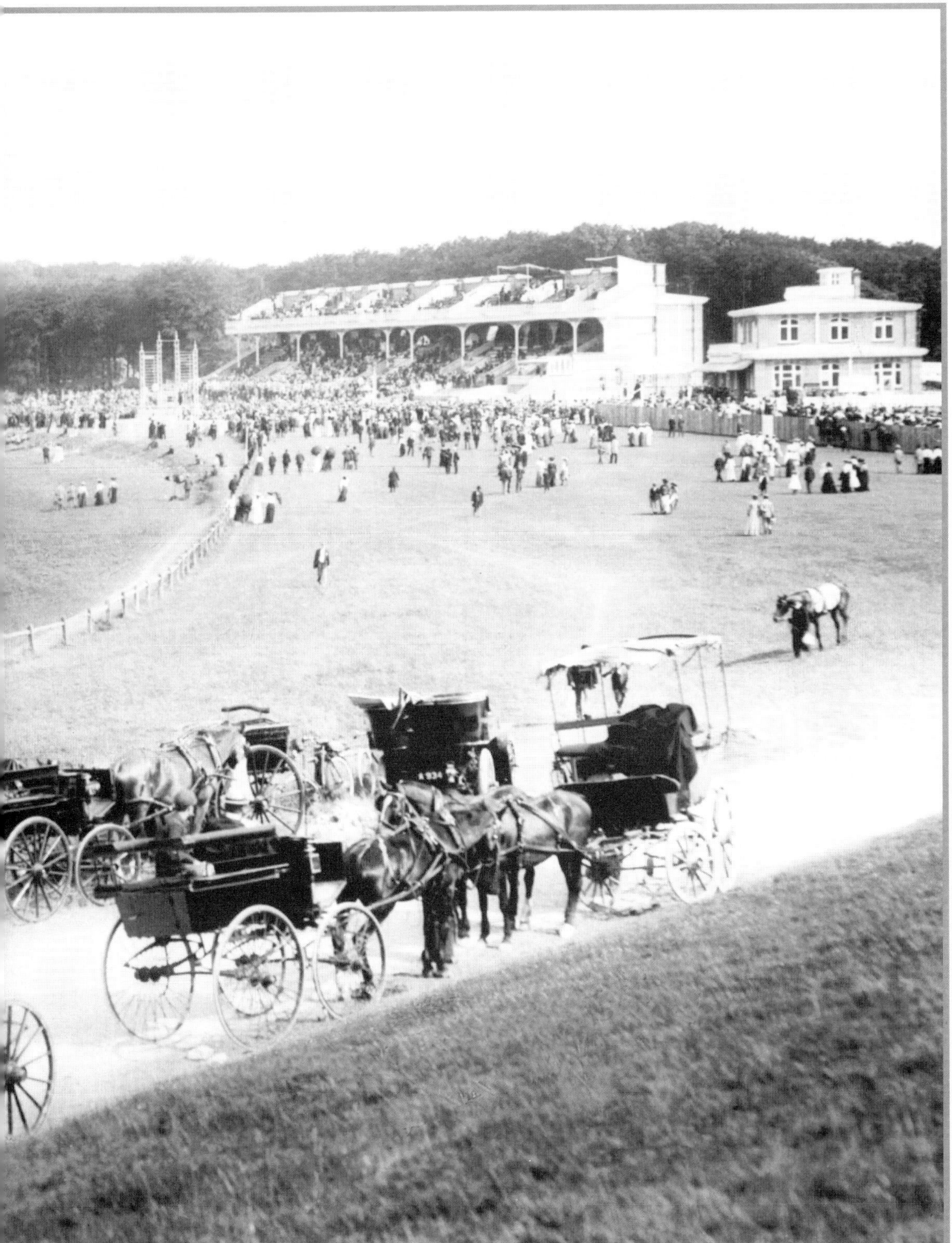

GOODWOOD HOUSE, THE RACECOURSE 1904 52295
This view shows the splendid new grandstand which had just been opened for this 1904 season. A jaunty two-decker, it has since been replaced by very modern grandstands of exceptional architectural quality. They do full justice to the July five-day meeting, held every year since 1814 and a key event in the English social calendar.

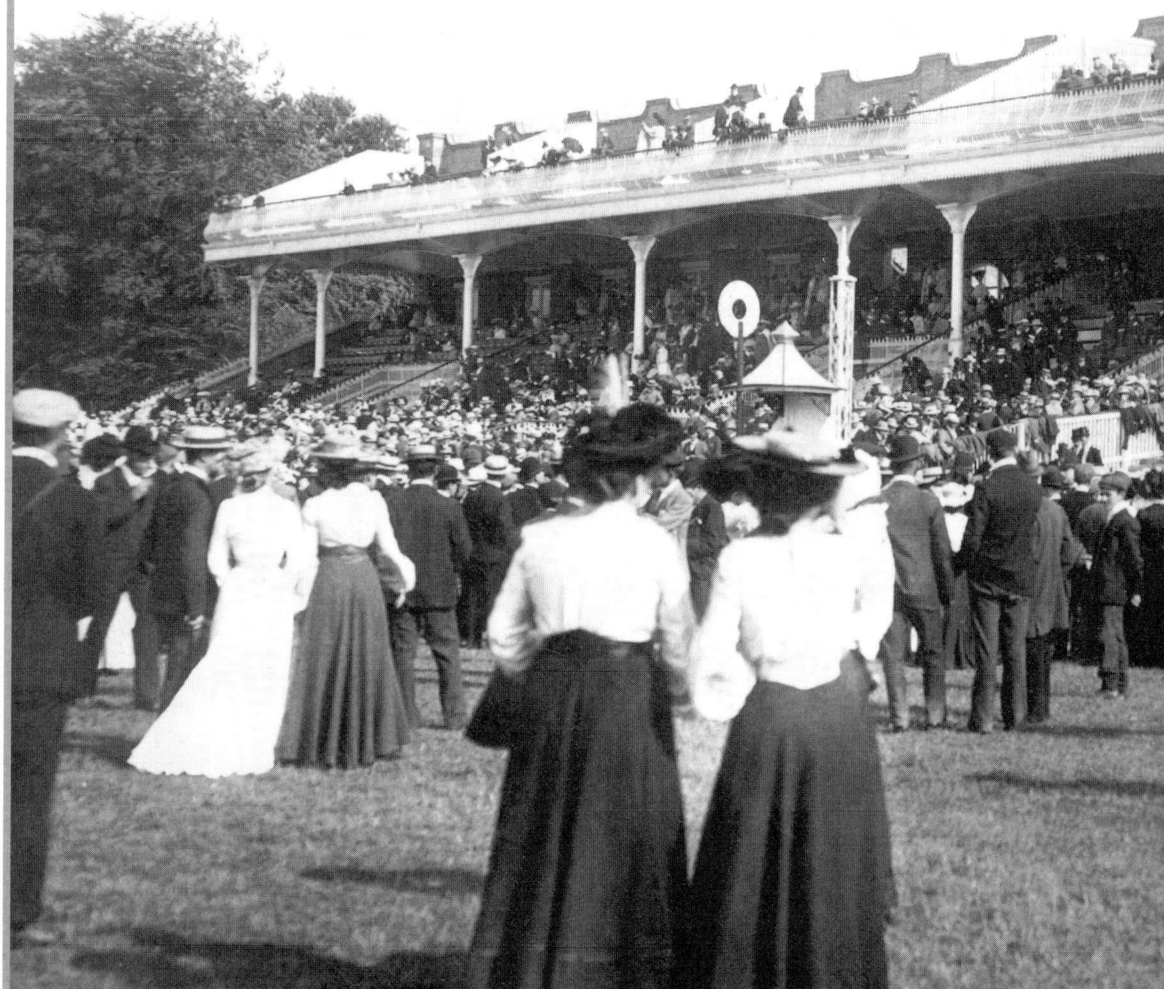

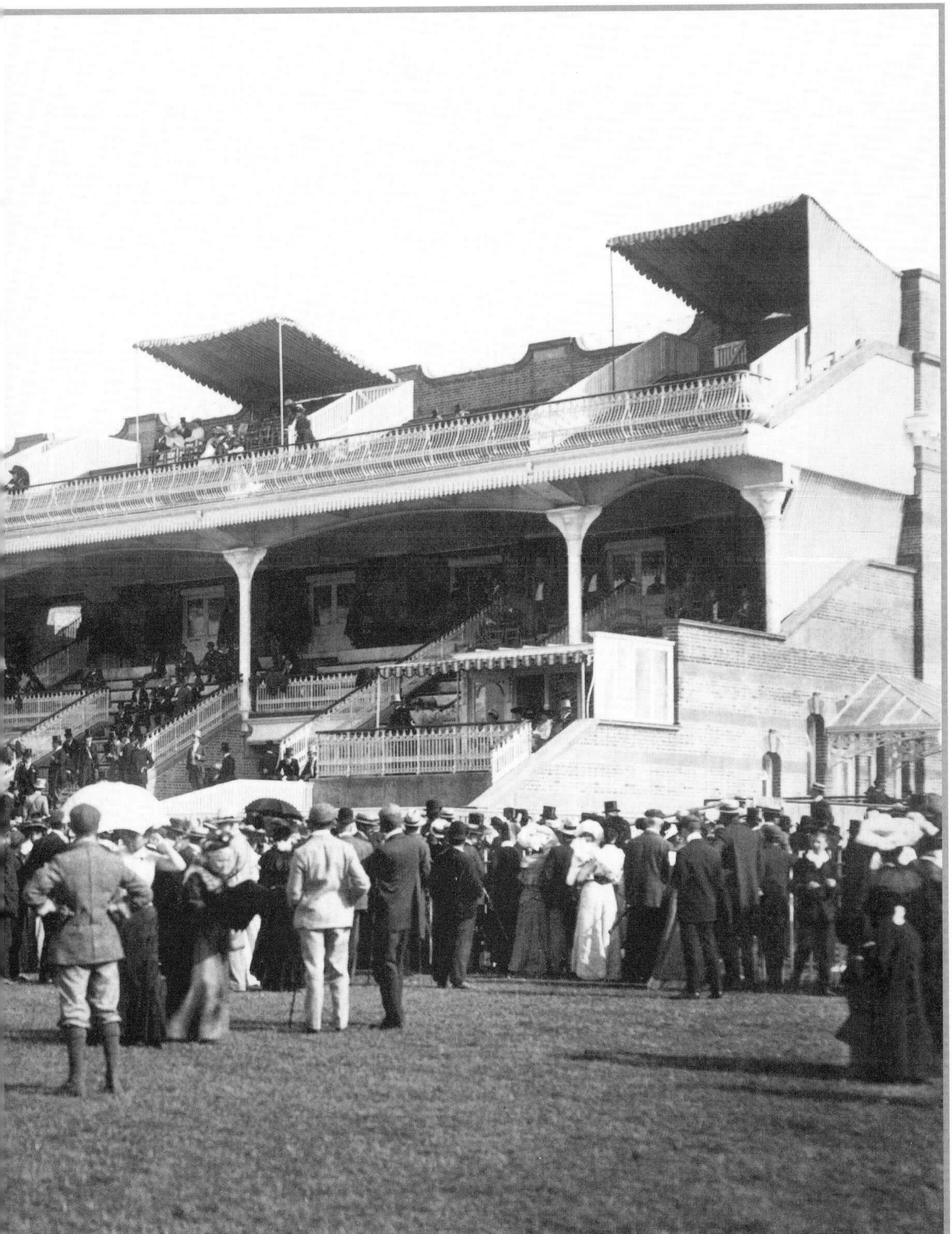

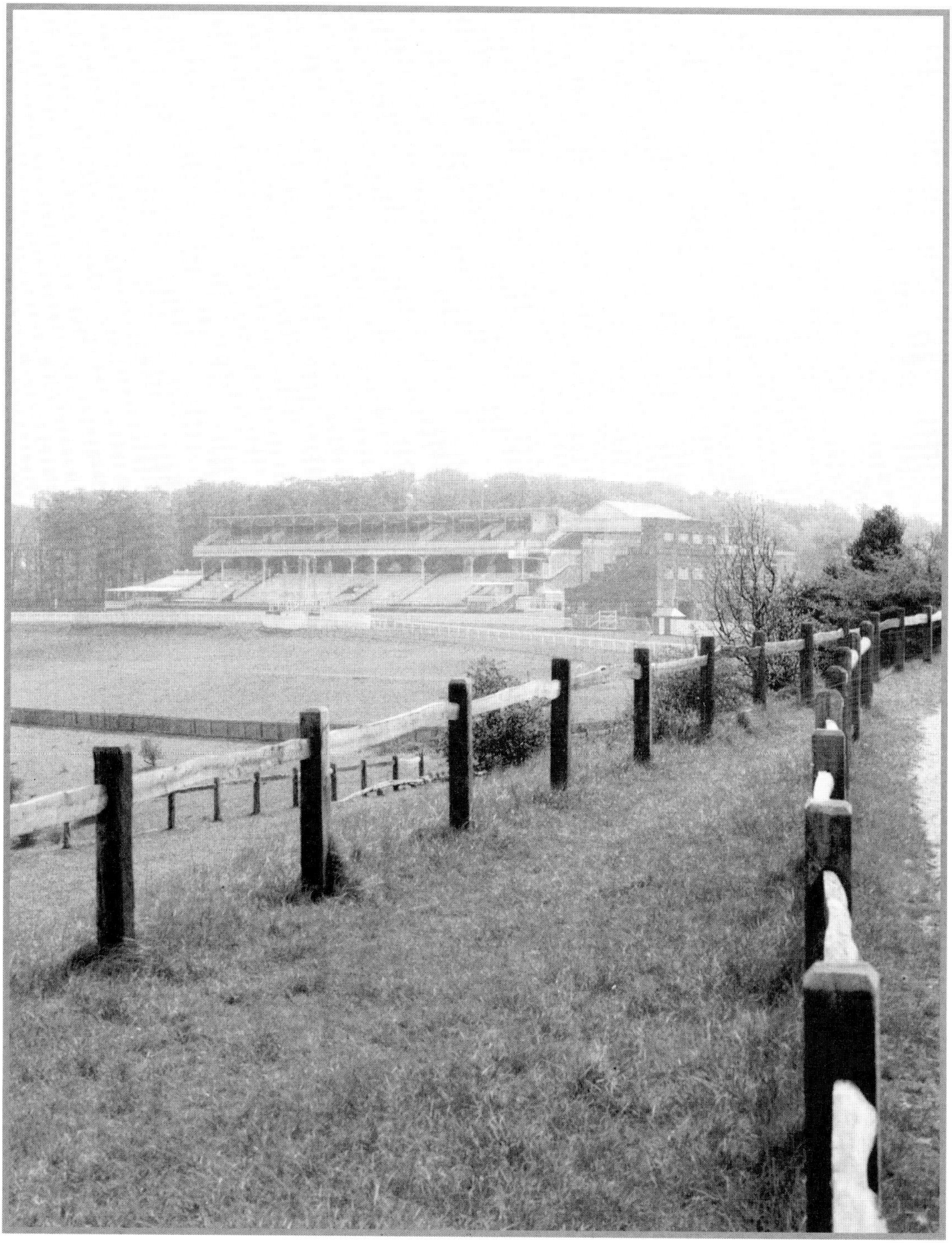

GOODWOOD RACE COURSE c1955 C84020

This atmospheric view shows the grandstand in its later days with a backdrop of beech woodland. It was designed in 1904 by A J Henderson, an architect from Esher in Surrey who presumably knew Epsom race course. To the left, and well away from the finishing post by the main grandstand, is the public enclosure, which still survives.

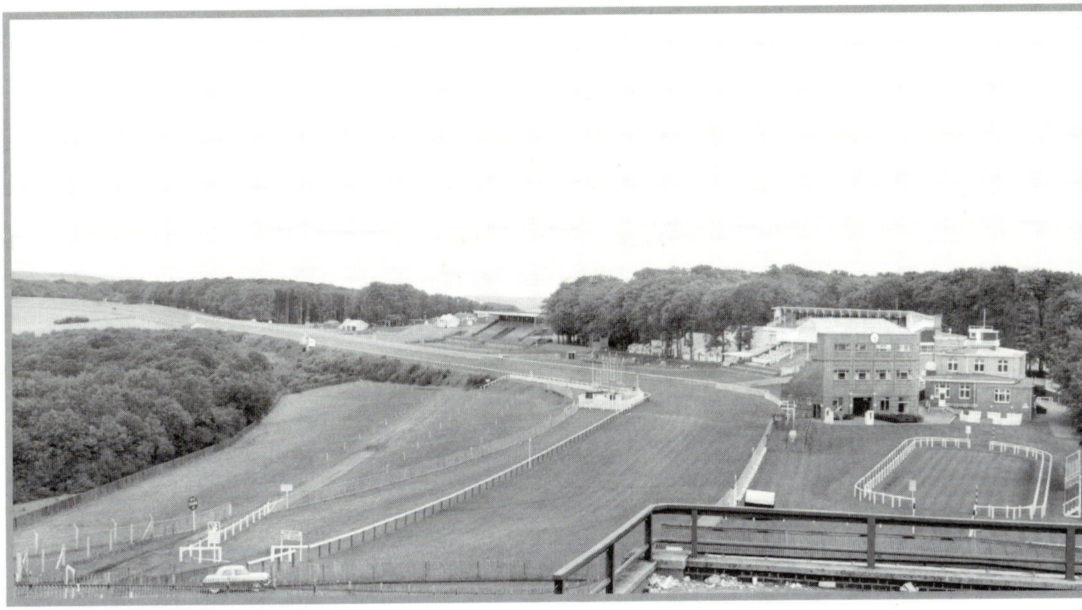

Goodwood Race Course c1960 C84078

This view of the immaculate race course is taken looking down from the slopes of St Roche's Hill which is surmounted by The Trundle, a spectacular Iron Age hill fort somewhat cluttered by communication masts. The then trendy two-tone Ford with whitewall tyres is on the road that soon turns south to descend to Goodwood House.

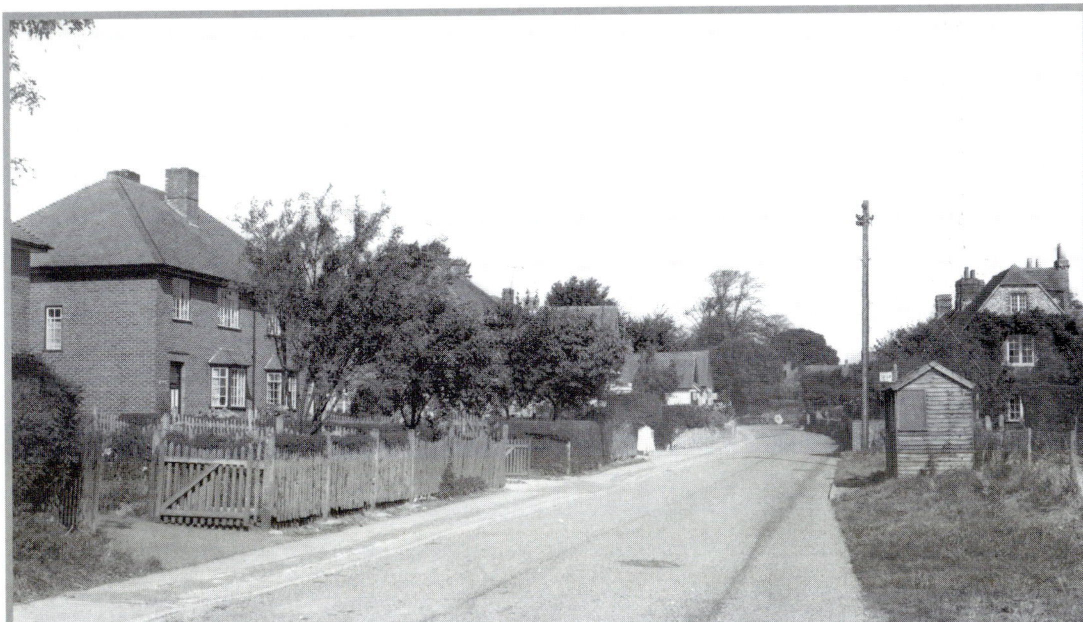

Boxgrove, The Street c1960 B167012

From Goodwood head for Boxgrove, a village that lies in a triangle south of the ancient Roman road that connected Chichester or Noviomagus Regnensium to London, and north of the present A27 Chichester to Arundel road. It is a linear street village, with the very fine priory church immediately to the east.

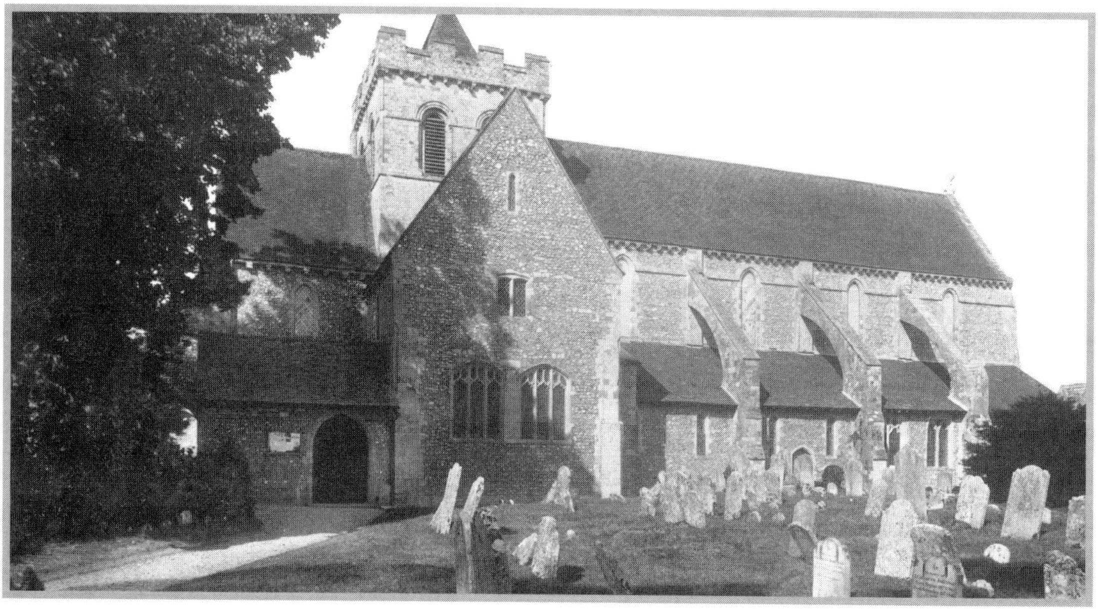

BOXGROVE, THE PRIORY 1899 44888
The priory was founded in about 1108 by Robert de la Haye as a 'priory' or daughter house of Lessay Abbey in the Cotentin peninsula of Normandy. In the early 13th century the Norman chancel was demolished and replaced by a splendid and larger Early English Gothic one, copying the 1180s choir of what is now Portsmouth Cathedral.

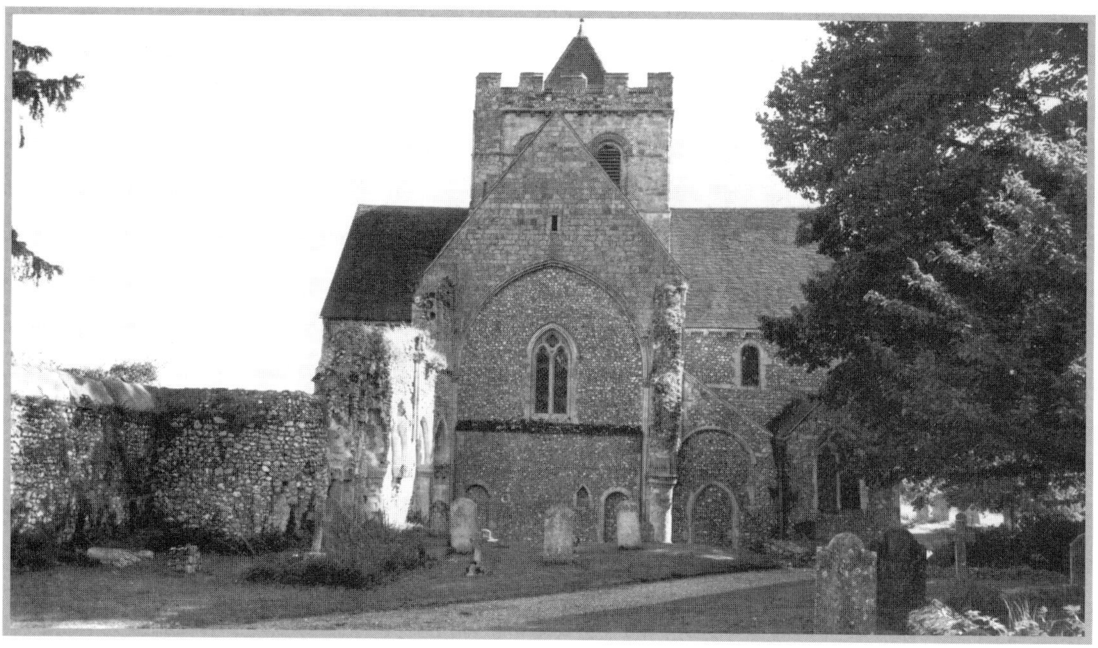

BOXGROVE, THE PRIORY c1960 B167004
This view is taken within the site of the late 12th-century nave. This was added on to the two bays of the monks' Norman nave, which was separated from the laity by the stone wall below the window. After the Priory was dissolved in 1536 the parishioners moved into the monks' church and demolished the nave.

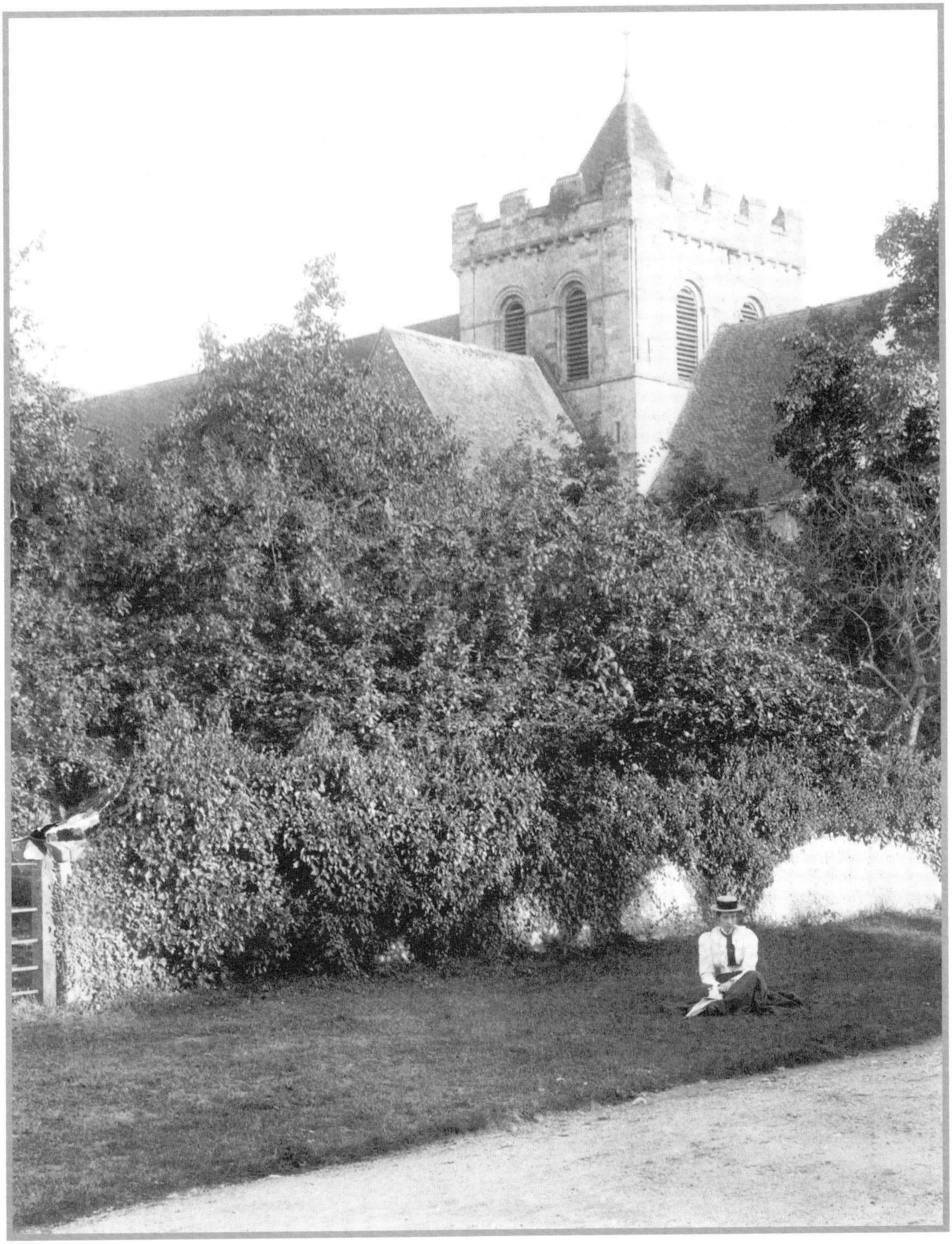

Boxgrove, The Priory 1899 44890

The crossing tower was remodelled in about 1170. This view shows the higher choir roof on the left and the lower north transept and nave roofs on the right. The wall is now cleared of vegetation to reveal the chapter house's arcaded front wall of about 1130, recently well restored.

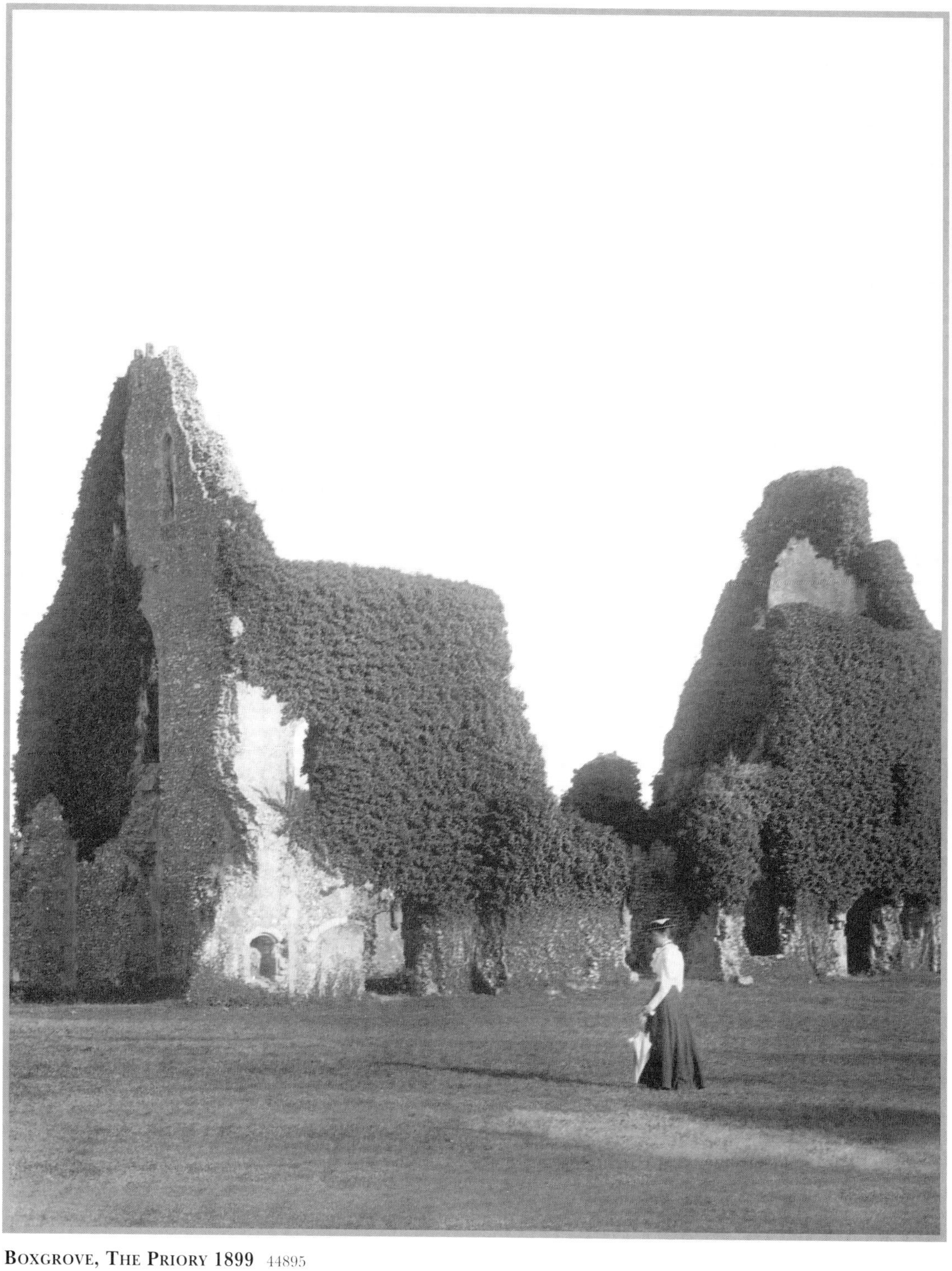

BOXGROVE, THE PRIORY 1899 44895
All of the priory buildings have long gone, except for the Guest House. This, dating from about 1300, was of two storeys with a vaulted undercroft and a substantial fireplace in the upper hall. In this view it is choked in ivy. It is now a much cleaner and consolidated ruin surrounded by a fence.

Boxgrove
The Village c1960
Originally a track leading west from the village into its open fields, Crouch Cross Lane was laid out for Chichester Rural District Council housing in the 1950s, though most are now owner-occupied. It is something of a mystery why Frith should make a postcard of such a subject, but the Morris Minor and the Austin A30 certainly add a period flavour.

Boxgrove
The Village c1960
The village's main north-south street is, unoriginally, named The Street. In this view is a terrace of three typical early 19th-century brick labourers' cottages and, beyond the turning into Crouch Cross Lane, further cottages and the Victorian village school.

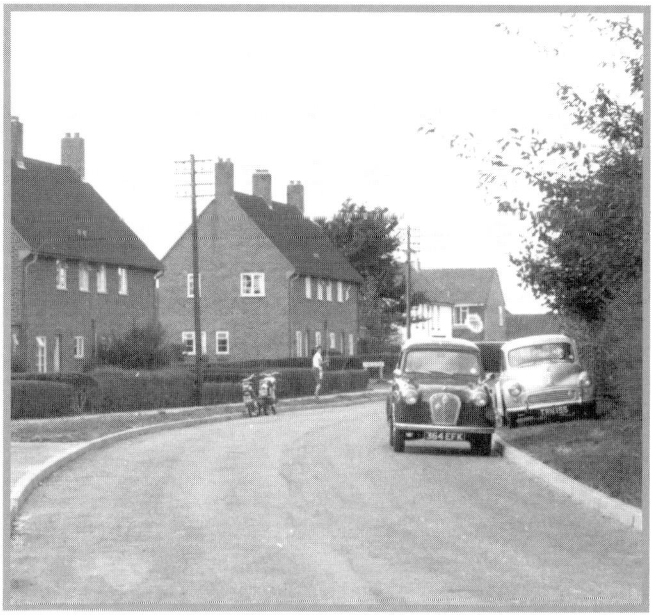

Boxgrove, The Village c1960 B167010

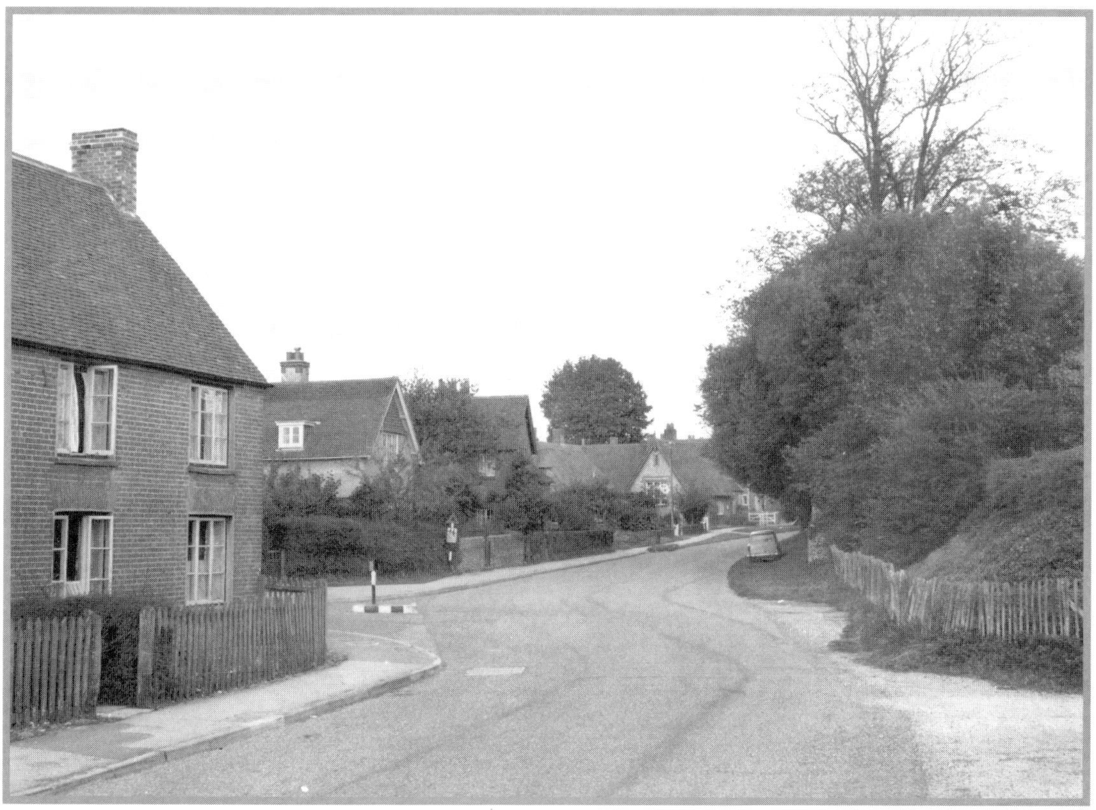

Boxgrove, The Village c1960 B167011

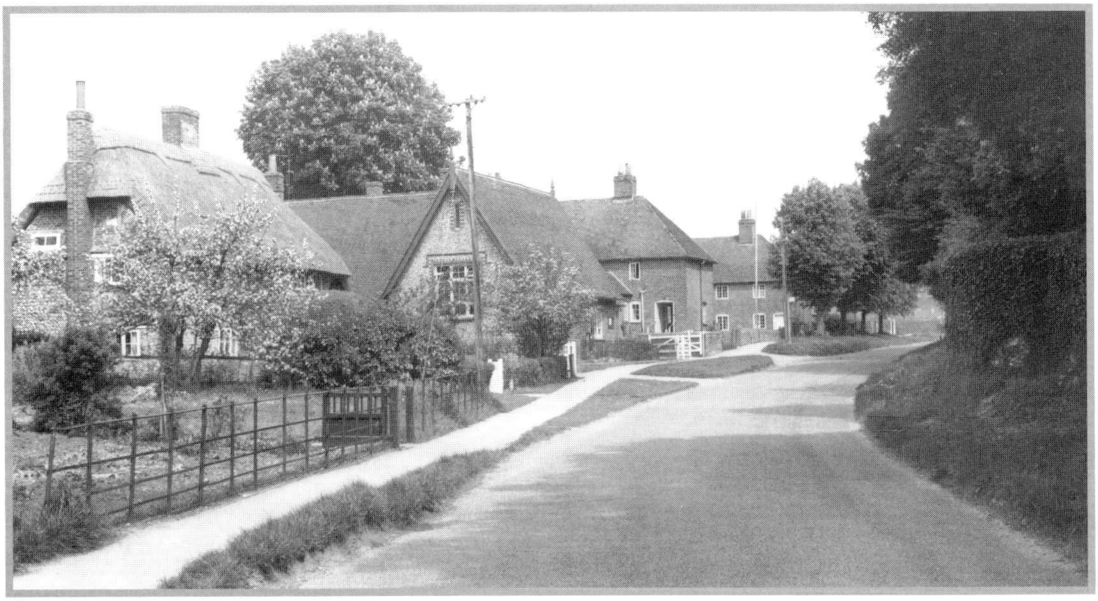

BOXGROVE, THE VILLAGE c1960 B167027

North just beyond the Crouch Cross Lane junction is Boxgrove's best cottage, the thatched Nightingale Cottage, built during the Civil War and dated 1647, a felicitous mix of timber-framing, flint and weatherboarding. Beyond the school are the brick-built Derby Almshouses of about 1740, a three sided courtyard with a taller more ornate centrepiece.

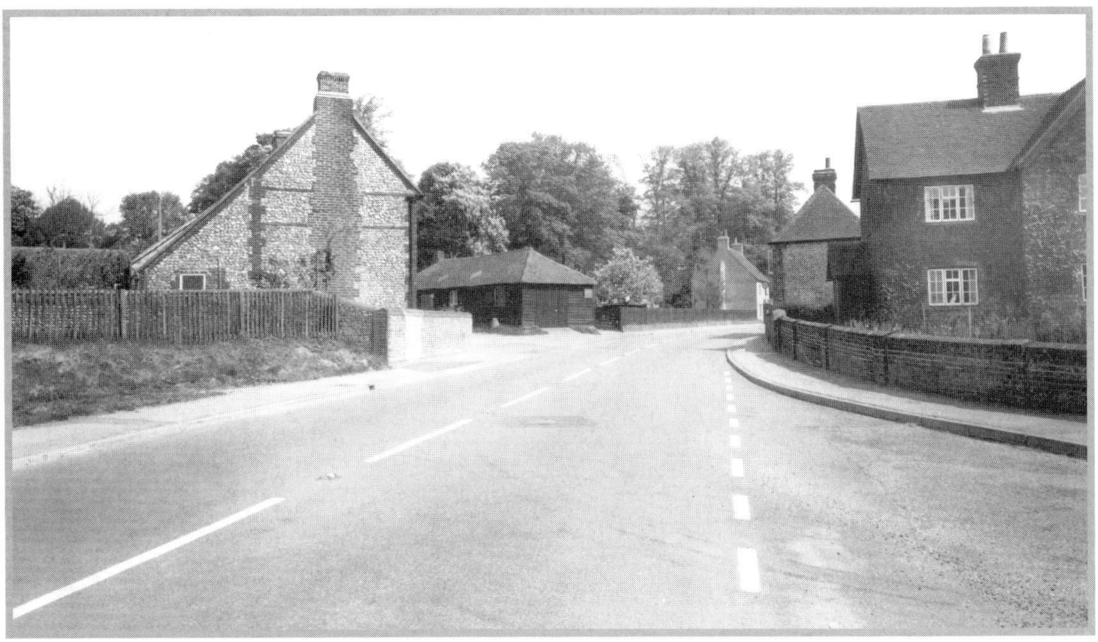

BOXGROVE, HALNAKER CORNER c1960 B167020

North of Boxgrove village the road reaches the crossroads at Halnaker, a hamlet on the old Roman road to Chichester with a further road leading west into the Goodwood estate. Beyond the flint gable of Rose Cottage on the left is the weatherboarded Blacksmith's Shop, still working.

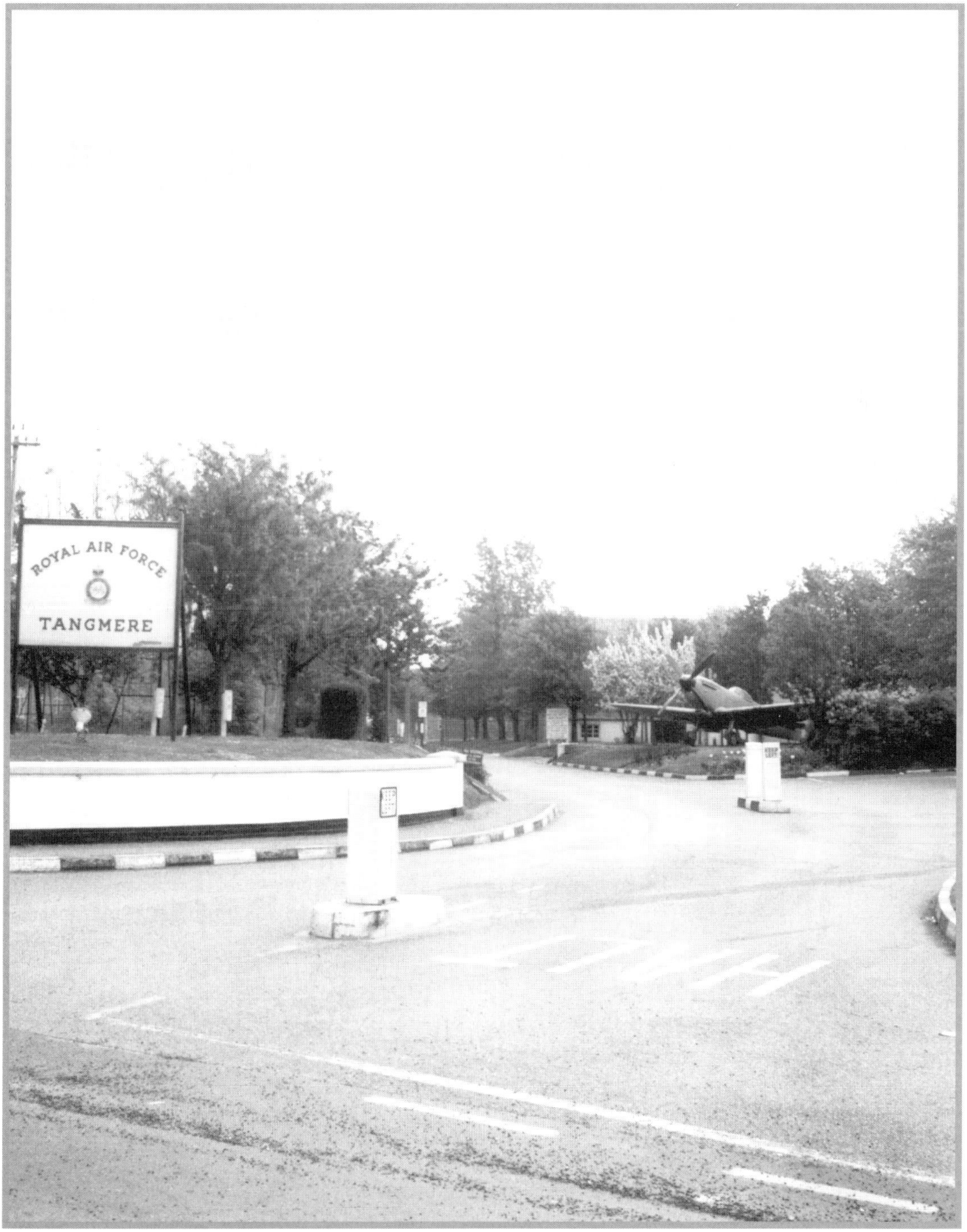

BOXGROVE, ENTRANCE TO RAF AERODROME, TANGMERE c1960 B167016
Tangmere Aerodrome's Hurricanes and Spitfires played a crucial role in the Battle of Britain, shooting down many German bombers and their escorting fighters; Douglas Bader was a Wing Commander here. Its illustrious history, that started in 1918 during World War I, ended when the aerodrome closed in 1970, to be replaced by a housing estate.

Index

Frith Book Co 1999 Titles

From 2000 we aim at publishing 100 new books each year. For latest catalogue please contact Frith Book Co

Barnstaple	1-85937-084-5	£12.99	Oct 99
Blackpool	1-85937-049-7	£12.99	Sep 99
Bognor Regis	1-85937-055-1	£12.99	Sep 99
Bristol	1-85937-050-0	£12.99	Sep 99
Cambridge	1-85937-092-6	£12.99	Oct 99
Cambridgeshire	1-85937-086-1	£14.99	Nov 99
Cheshire	1-85937-045-4	£14.99	Sep 99
Chester	1-85937-090-X	£12.99	Nov 99
Chesterfield	1-85937-071-3	£12.99	Sep 99
Chichester	1-85937-089-6	£12.99	Nov 99
Cornwall	1-85937-054-3	£14.99	Sep 99
Cotswolds	1-85937-099-3	£14.99	Nov 99

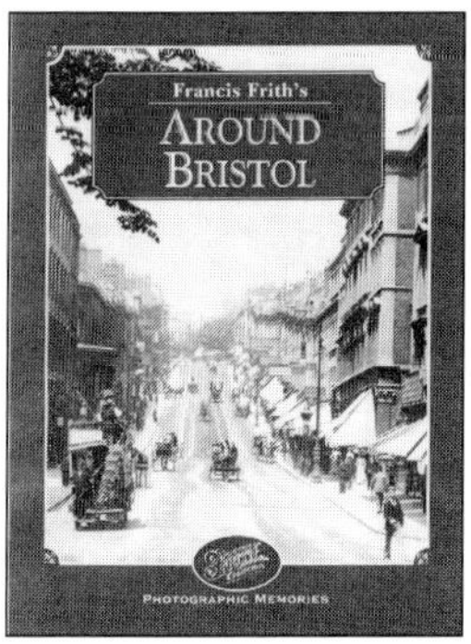

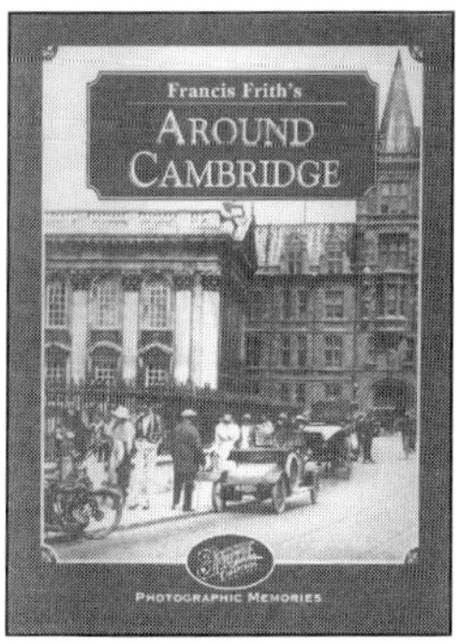

Derby	1-85937-046-2	£12.99	Sep 99
Devon	1-85937-052-7	£14.99	Sep 99
Dorset	1-85937-075-6	£14.99	Oct 99
Dorset Coast	1-85937-062-4	£14.99	Sep 99
Dublin	1-85937-058-6	£12.99	Sep 99
East Anglia	1-85937-059-4	£14.99	Sep 99
Eastbourne	1-85937-061-6	£12.99	Sep 99
English Castles	1-85937-078-0	£14.99	Oct 99
Essex	1-85937-082-9	£14.99	Nov 99
Falmouth	1-85937-066-7	£12.99	Sep 99
Hampshire	1-85937-064-0	£14.99	Sep 99
Hertfordshire	1-85937-079-9	£14.99	Nov 99
Isle of Man	1-85937-065-9	£14.99	Sep 99
Liverpool	1-85937-051-9	£12.99	Sep 99
Maidstone	1-85937-056-X	£12.99	Sep 99
Northumberland & Tyne and Wear	1-85937-072-1	£14.99	Sep 99
North Yorkshire	1-85937-048-9	£14.99	Sep 99
Nottingham	1-85937-060-8	£12.99	Sep 99
Oxfordshire	1-85937-076-4	£14.99	Oct 99
Penzance	1-85937-069-1	£12.99	Sep 99
Reading	1-85937-087-X	£12.99	Nov 99
St Ives	1-85937-068-3	£12.99	Sep 99
Salisbury	1-85937-091-8	£12.99	Nov 99
Scarborough	1-85937-104-3	£12.99	Sep 99
Scottish Castles	1-85937-077-2	£14.99	Oct 99
Sevenoaks and Tonbridge	1-85937-057-8	£12.99	Sep 99
Sheffield and S Yorkshire	1-85937-070-5	£12.99	Sep 99
Shropshire	1-85937-083-7	£14.99	Nov 99
Southampton	1-85937-088-8	£12.99	Nov 99
Staffordshire	1-85937-047-0	£14.99	Sep 99
Stratford upon Avon	1-85937-098-5	£12.99	Nov 99
Suffolk	1-85937-074-8	£14.99	Oct 99
Surrey	1-85937-081-0	£14.99	Oct 99
Torbay	1-85937-063-2	£12.99	Sep 99
Wiltshire	1-85937-053-5	£14.99	Sep 99

British Life A Century Ago

246 x 189mm 144pp, hardback. Black and white

Lavishly illustrated with photos from the turn of the century, and with extensive commentary. It offers a unique insight into the social history and heritage of bygone Britain.

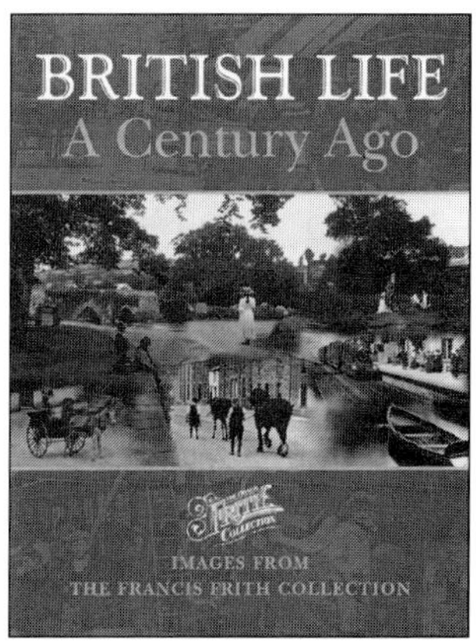

1-85937-103-5 £17.99

Available from your local bookshop or from the publisher

Frith Products & Services

Francis Frith would doubtless be pleased to know that the pioneering publishing venture he started in 1860 still continues today. More than a hundred and thirty years later, The Francis Frith Collection continues in the same innovative tradition and is now one of the foremost publishers of vintage photographs in the world. Some of the current activities include:

Interior Decoration

Today Frith's photographs can be seen framed and as giant wall murals in thousands of pubs, restaurants, hotels, banks, retail stores and other public buildings throughout the country. In every case they enhance the unique local atmosphere of the places they depict and provide reminders of gentler days in an increasingly busy and frenetic world.

Product Promotions

Frith products have been used by many major companies to promote the sales of their own products or to reinforce their own history and heritage. Brands include Hovis bread, Courage beers, Scots Porage Oats, Colman's mustard, Cadbury's foods, Mellow Birds coffee, Dunhill pipe tobacco, Guinness, and Bulmer's Cider.

Genealogy and Family History

As the interest in family history and roots grows world-wide, more and more people are turning to Frith's photographs of Great Britain for images of the towns, villages and streets where their ancestors lived; and, of course, photographs of the churches and chapels where their ancestors were christened, married and buried are an essential part of every genealogy tree and family album.

A series of easy-to-use CD Roms is planned for publication, and an increasing number of Frith photographs will be able to be viewed on specialist genealogy sites. A growing range of Frith books will be available on CD.

The Internet

Already thousands of Frith photographs can be viewed and purchased on the internet. By the end of the year 2000 some 60,000 Frith photographs will be available on the internet. The number of sites is constantly expanding, each focussing on different products and services from the Collection.

Some of the sites are listed below.

www.townpages.co.uk
www.familystorehouse.com
www.britannia.com
www.icollector.com
www.barclaysquare.co.uk
www.cornwall-online.co.uk

For background information on the Collection look at the two following sites:

www.francisfrith.com
www.francisfrith.co.uk

Frith Products

All Frith photographs are available Framed or just as Mounted Prints, and can be ordered from the address below. From time to time other products - Address Books, Calendars, Table Mats, Postcards etc - are available.

The Frith Collectors' Guild

In response to the many customers who enjoy collecting Frith photographs we have created the Frith Collectors' Guild. Members are entitled to a range of benefits, including a regular magazine, special discounts and special limited edition products.

For further information: if you would like further information on any of the above aspects of the Frith business please contact us at the address below:

The Francis Frith Collection, Frith's Barn, Teffont, Salisbury, Wiltshire England SP3 5QP.

Tel: +44 (0) 1722 716 376 Fax: +44 (0) 1722 716 881 Email: frithbook.co.uk

To receive your FREE Mounted Print

Cut out this Voucher and return it with your remittance for £1.50 to cover postage and handling. Choose any photograph included in this book. Your SEPIA print will be A4 in size, and mounted in a cream mount with burgundy rule lines, overall size 14 x 11 inches.

Order additional Mounted Prints at HALF PRICE (only £7.49 each*)
If there are further pictures you would like to order, possibly as gifts for friends and family, acquire them at half price (no additional postage and handling required).

Have your Mounted Prints framed*
For an additional £14.95 per print you can have your chosen Mounted Print framed in an elegant polished wood and gilt moulding, overall size 16 x 13 inches (no additional postage and handling required).

*** IMPORTANT!**
These special prices are only available if ordered using the original voucher on this page (no copies permitted) and at the same time as your free Mounted Print, for delivery to the same address

Voucher for FREE and Reduced Price Frith Prints

Picture no.	Page number	Qty	Mounted @ £7.49	Framed + £14.95	Total Cost
		1	**Free of charge***	£	£
			£	£	£
			£	£	£
			£	£	£
			£	£	£
			£	£	£
				* Post & handling	£1.50
				Total Order Cost	**£**

Title: AROUND PENZANCE

069-1

Please do not photocopy this voucher. Only the original is valid, so please cut it out and return it to us.

I enclose a cheque / postal order for £ . . . .
made payable to 'The Francis Frith Collection'
OR please debit my Mastercard / Visa / Switch / Amex card

Number . . . .

Expires . . . . Signature . . . .

Name Mr/Mrs/Ms ....

Address ....

....

....

....

.... Postcode ....

Daytime Tel No ....

Valid to 31/12/01

Frith Collectors' Guild

From time to time we publish a magazine of news and stories about Frith photographs and further special offers of Frith products. If you would like 12 months FREE membership, please return this form and we will send you a New Member Pack.

The Francis Frith Collectors' Guild

I would like to receive the New Members Pack offering 12 months FREE membership.

069-1

Name Mr/Mrs/Ms ....

Address ....

....

....

.... Postcode ....

Send completed forms to:
The Francis Frith Collection, Frith's Barn, Teffont, Salisbury, Wiltshire SP3 5QP